NO RESERVATIONS,
NO RETREATS,
NO REGRETS

OMS · ONE MISSION SOCIETY

By God's grace, One Mission Society unites, inspires, and equips Christians to make disciples of Jesus Christ, multiplying dynamic communities of believers around the world.

One Mission Society is an evangelical, interdenominational faith mission that makes disciples of Jesus Christ through intentional evangelism, planting churches, forming strategic partnerships, and training national leaders in Africa, Asia, the Caribbean, Europe, Latin America, and the Middle East. One Mission Society then joins with those churches in global partnerships to reach the rest of the world.

One Mission Society
PO Box A
Greenwood, IN 46142
317.888.3333
www.onemissionsociety.org
http://oms.media

NO RESERVES, NO RETREATS, NO REGRETS

The Early Life and Ministry of Ed Erny

By Ed Erny

No Reserves, No Retreats, No Regrets - Ed Erny
Copyright © 2015 by One Mission Society

One Mission Society
PO Box A
Greenwood, IN 46142
317.888.3333
www.onemissionsociety.org
http://oms.media

Paperback ISBN: 978-1-62245-279-8
eBook ISBN: 978-1-62245-280-4

Cover design by W. Foster Pilcher.

Scripture quotations marked "KJV" are taken from the Holy Bible, King James Version, Cambridge, 1769.

All Scripture quotations, unless otherwise indicated, are taken from the Holy Bible, New International Version®, NIV®. Copyright ©1973, 1978, 1984, by Biblica, Inc.™ Used by permission of Zondervan. All rights reserved worldwide. www.zondervan.com

All rights reserved. No part of this book may be reproduced in any form without permission in writing from the publisher, except in the case of brief quotations in critical articles or reviews.

BIOGRAPHY & AUTOBIOGRAPHY / Religious

Printed in the United States of America
10 9 8 7 6 5 4 3 2 1

Contents

FOREWORD VII
CH 1: ONE DIVINE MOMENT 1
CH 2: INDIA 13
CH 3: A NEW ENVIRONMENT 23
CH 4: YOSEMITE 29
CH 5: ROUTE 66 TO ASBURY COLLEGE 41
CH 6: MY FIRST PREACHING 49
CH 7: CAMPUS ACTIVITIES 57
CH 8: SHELBYVILLE 63
CH 9: A NEW CHALLENGE 71
CH 10: A NEW COMPANION 77
CH 11: SEMINARY 85
CH 12: ENGAGED 91
CH 13: FUNDING 105
CH 14: SPIRITUAL INSIGHTS 115
CH 15: THE VOYAGE 129
CH 16: JAPAN 139
CH 17: FORMOSA WELCOME 149
CH 18: FIRST IMPRESSIONS 159
CH 19: YUANLIN 167
CH 20: A MINISTRY BEGUN 175
CH 21: TOULIU 185
CH 22: "YE SHALL BEAR FRUIT" 193
CH 23: TAINAN AND BEYOND 201
CH 24: HUALIEN AND HONG KONG 209
CH 25: THE DELUGE 217
CH 26: CHANGHUA 223
CH 27: CHIAYI AND HOME 231
EPILOGUE 247

FOREWORD

This volume does not contain my full and complete autobiography – far from it. In defense of this detailed recounting of the first twenty-three years of my life, I offer a sort of rationale.

Psychologists agree that the first twenty-some years of a person's life are without a doubt the most important and influential years of our earthly sojourn. Almost all of man's important choices are made during this period, choices relative to family relations, education, employment, marriage, and children. For many, this brief block of time represents the single most important and significant period of our life on this earth. And above all, often during these years we answer life's greatest question: What shall I do with Jesus?

I was born in the thirty-sixth year of a century that includes the two bloodiest wars in human history. In God's mercy, my father, who entered active service in World War I, avoided by a matter of months being sent to the conflict in the fields of Europe. Had he died there, as so many of his generation did, our entire family and progeny would have disappeared into oblivion. I am grateful this was not God's plan.

The twentieth century was a period of time without parallel in human history, an explosion of incredible proportions in which tidal waves of knowledge and invention swept over the human race. One can only mention a few of the major world-changing inventions. Transportation and communication were altered with the mass production of the automobile, airplanes, telephones, and electric lights and power, altering every phase of human behavior and achievement. Amazing medical know-how and medications by the score, during the brief compass of my lifetime, have lengthened man's life on planet earth by an average of twenty years or more. Technology has thrust upon us inventions so prolific it boggles the mind to even keep abreast of a changing world. All of this has come in a comparative sliver of human time. And that encompasses my lifespan.

The title I chose for this book includes words written by William Borden, heir to the Borden fortune, at different times in his short life. After graduating from Yale University, he went to Egypt to study Arabic, having been called to be a missionary to Muslims. In 1913, while there he contracted spinal meningitis and died. Shortly before his death at the age of twenty-five, he wrote the last of the three phrases, "No Regrets."

I hope upon the completion of this volume to write a second and final part of the story. In all this and for the great grace bestowed upon me, I write these words: To God be the glory!

Ed Erny
Greenwood, Indiana
2013

CHAPTER 1

ONE DIVINE MOMENT

In the spring of 1958, God visited the campus of Asbury College (now Asbury University) with revival of the sort I had often heard about, but had never seen. During its history, the college witnessed four of these spiritual earthquakes.

According to E. Stanley Jones, one of Asbury's most famous alumni, the first of the revivals occurred in 1914 when he was a student in the small ministerial college. "Before it was over," said Jones, "every single person in Wilmore [a village of about two thousand at the time] confessed Christ as Savior."

The second great spontaneous revival erupted in 1950 during a chapel service in which a campus leader felt compelled to make a confession of sin, hypocrisy, and coldness of heart. Classmates followed him to the long altar that extends across the front of Hughes Auditorium. Shortly thereafter, happy shouts of "Praise God" and "Hallelujah" could be heard by passersby on Lexington Avenue, the central highway that separates Asbury College from Asbury Theological Seminary.

Regular classes were suspended as unscheduled services continued all night and into the following day. The senior class play planned for that weekend was postponed indefinitely. Students who had experienced salvation or personal revival during the events of that first day began calling parents and friends all over the U.S. The result was scores of hastily organized pilgrimages to the precincts of Asbury College where, without a doubt, a kind of sacred bush was burning. Some called the campus "holy ground." Men of worldly mind and fleshly disposition acknowledged suddenly falling under conviction when they set foot on the semicircle that fronts the college and is bordered by tall antebellum columns.

The secular press, though not easily impressed by reports of religious movements in the Bible Belt, soon became aware of unusual goings-on and dispatched newsmen to Asbury College. Associated Press and United Press International reporters showed up, and by week's end the Asbury College revival was a top news story throughout the U.S., second only to the current steel strike. The 1950 revival then spread as deputation teams were dispatched to other colleges and churches throughout the eastern and central states and as far west as Los Angeles.

When I arrived in 1954 as a sophomore on the campus of Asbury, the talk of the great 1950 revival was still circulating. Eyewitnesses, some converts of the 1950 movement, were now employed on campus. When they spoke of the divine moment, there was awe in their voices and a glow on their faces.

Asbury College was named for America's father of Methodism, the great circuit rider Francis Asbury. The college was established in 1890, thanks to the vision of a Methodist minister, John Wesley Hughes. By this time, the inroads of German higher criticism, with its attendant liberalism, had resulted in the gradual departure of the Methodist Church from its early Wesleyan moorings. It was in protest to this trend and in order to preserve the true evangelical faith that Hughes had built a small, clapboard, twelve-by-fifty-foot building to house his new school. Its singular purpose was to train ministers, missionaries, and church workers to fortify the old Methodist foundations.

I have often wondered what direction my life would have taken had it not been for Asbury College and Seminary. The chain of circumstances that had guided me that fall afternoon from my home in Los Angeles, twenty-four hundred miles away, to the undulating hills of Kentucky went back to the 1920s.

My father, Eugene Erny, was the son of Swiss immigrants who had fled to the United States in the 1880s to escape Bismarck's conscriptions. The Ernys had for generations lived in the Swiss hamlet of Gelterkinden, outside of Basel, and settled in Racine, Wisconsin, where my father was born.

Though the Ernys had been bakers in Switzerland, in their new home they first pursued truck farming and then built a factory that produced furniture and other wood products, particularly baskets. In this pre-cardboard-box era, baskets were in great demand for shipping all sorts of foodstuffs and breakables, such as china and porcelain. In time, the Badger Company became a major supplier of Marshall Field's department store, as well as the burgeoning Kraft Food Company. Though the factory remained in Wisconsin, in time, the family moved the company offices to Chicago and settled in an upscale suburb.

The family members were proper Swiss-German Protestants, religiously devout and members of a large denominational church. All of this, for some reason, never fully satisfied the spiritual yearnings of my grandmother, Mary Erny. When some friends, members of a new denomination called the Nazarenes, invited her to a camp meeting, she readily accepted. Here for the first time, Mary heard impassioned preaching on the glorious blessings and necessity of being filled with the Holy Spirit, also described as "being sanctified." This experience, she was told, eventuated in scriptural holiness and a victorious life freed from the power of sin.

What the family discovered, to their consternation, was that Mother had come back from the camp meeting a disturbingly different woman. Her face shone with a strange sort of light. Moreover, she now had a passion for prayer, not merely the calm ritual of prayer that they were accustomed to, but shamelessly impassioned prayer, punctuated by sighs, groans, and occasional outbursts of praise.

The change manifested itself in other even more alarming ways. Mary Erny took an interest in city missions, derelicts, and women of ill repute. On occasion, she invited these ladies to her home to love them, pray with them, and hopefully lead them to the Savior.

This sort of fanaticism disturbed the household routine and introduced activities with which the family was not altogether comfortable. Above all, Mary now made it known that she was praying for her children, asking that God would fill them with His Holy Spirit and that they would offer themselves for Christian service, preferably as ministers or missionaries.

While most of the family continued faithful attendance at the Baptist church, Mary began worshiping in a holiness mission called Austin Tabernacle, an assembly so enthusiastic in their worship that none of the other Ernys ever felt comfortable in the fellowship. Here, during testimony times and Wednesday night prayer meetings, Mary would tearfully request prayer for her offspring, beginning with "my oldest son, Eugene."

In many ways, these were difficult days for the family. Eugene Sr. (for whom my father was named), head of the clan and the business, was stricken with encephalitis. His movement was impaired, and he lost control of facial muscles on his left side. Dad, now twenty-one, had been drafted by the military in 1918. But following the World War I armistice in November of that year, he returned home to take over management of the family business.

Under his direction, the company did well financially. His future seemed secure and for the family things looked hopeful and stable.

Dad, however, did not long remain satisfied in his new role

as head of the family business. In the following months, he gradually began to sense that God was leading him into the ministry. This change of life direction was finalized dramatically one particular evening.

"It was a Wednesday night," I often heard Dad recall, "and I had been working late at the office. I looked at my watch, and it was almost 7:30, the time the prayer meeting at Austin Tabernacle usually let out." There had always been a special tie between young Eugene and his mother. Now, on an impulse, he decided to go home by way of the tabernacle, meet his mother, and take her home in the Pierce Arrow, the car that was a symbol of the family's success.

As it turned out, when Eugene slipped into a pew at the back of the small church, the service had not yet concluded and his mother was nowhere in sight. Not wishing to draw attention to himself, Dad decided to wait until after the benediction to leave. Though young Eugene knew few of the worshipers in the small tabernacle, many of the people, including the minister, somehow recognized him as the oldest son of Mary Erny, the boy for whom she had often requested prayer.

The minister, seeing Eugene at the back, paused and then continued, "I feel that we cannot close this service yet. I believe there is someone here with a spiritual need. If so, we invite you to come to the altar as we sing a song of invitation." Though the church made a great deal of altar calls, they had not yet provided a proper kneeling bench. The makeshift altar was, in fact, only a few rickety chairs turned to face the congregation. Dad recalled that one of the chairs even suffered a broken slat. When no one responded to the invitation, the pastor interrupted with a slight amendment. "I just feel," he said, "that there is a young man here who has a spiritual need. If so, we will sing another verse and keep the altar open." Dad, his face hidden behind an open hymnal, glanced around at the small assembly.

He realized that he was the only young man present. Another verse of the invitation hymn was sung and then another. Finally, as though some divine hand were propelling him, on the final verse, Eugene moved out of his pew and down the aisle.

A group of the church members, commonly acknowledged as "the saints," gathered around young Eugene, praying softly, some placing hands of encouragement on his shoulders.

For months, Eugene had suspected that God might be calling him to preach. He was, in fact, the leader of his church's youth group and had preached many times, even in German. Still he argued, "I have been gifted by God as a businessman. I can serve Him much better as a major supporter of the church and can even take the lead in financing missionary projects." The struggle that followed at the altar continued for ten minutes, then twenty, then half an hour. Still there was no relief. He remembers that it was a full forty minutes before peace came. It was the peace of total, unconditional capitulation, a willingness to do anything and everything that God asked – yes, even to preach the gospel and become a minister or evangelist.

When Dad shared later that God had called him to preach, a young lady gave him this advice: "In that case, you must go to Asbury College in Kentucky."

When thirty-three years later I arrived on that picturesque campus, the gracious lawns shaded by black walnut trees, this was all familiar scenery to a generation of Ernys. Dad had enrolled and was later followed by three siblings: sisters, Jeanette and Florence, and his younger brother, Edward, for whom I am named. Uncle Bill, the only one who did not attend Asbury, became the successful executive of the family company.

Since Dad had never finished high school, upon enrolling in Asbury College in 1921, he completed his high school studies in the college academy while at the same time pursuing his BA degree. Older than most students on campus, Dad was a recognized leader almost from the start, and in his final year he was elected senior class president. He led in the funding of the class project, constructing a large water tower serving both the college and the city of Wilmore, an exceedingly ambitious undertaking for a small student body that consisted mostly of poor preacher boys.

During college, Eugene was known as a gifted basketball player, a sport he had learned at the Chicago YMCA. Though a short five foot eight, he was remarkably quick and accurate. He was the team captain and the coach. Their team record of but one loss in four years remains unmatched.

My father's photo in the 1925 yearbook shows a handsome and athletic young man flashing a broad grin that for him was as natural as breathing. Disconcerting, however, was that still in his twenties he was already seriously balding. He found some comfort in the fact that his good friend and classmate, Harold Best, suffered from the same affliction. During their years at Asbury, they experimented with a variety of nostrums, even a kind of black tar, all without success.

While on campus, Dad dated a number of popular girls but nothing serious materialized. His mother was soliciting prayer for her "aging" son who "has not yet found God's choice for him."

President H.C. Morrison came to regard Dad as a sort of protégé. He encouraged him and three classmates to spend summers in tent evangelism in central and eastern states. Dr. Morrison provided them with a large tent. During these summer campaigns, many were led to Christ and a considerable number of youth were encouraged to enroll in Asbury College.

When Dad graduated, he continued in evangelism with his heart set on one day pastoring a large tabernacle patterned after the one built by the famed Paul Rader in Chicago. This was the tabernacle that had, in fact, deeply influenced Eugene in his youth.

One of Dad's former classmates was a Korean boy named Robert Chung. Whenever Eugene met up with him, he prepared himself for Chung's fervent attempt at recruitment. "Eugene," Chung enthused, "you must come over to Korea and help us. In America, you have churches everywhere and pastors by the thousands. Most Koreans are still waiting to hear the gospel for the first time. You must come. I'll interpret for you and we'll spread the gospel all over Korea."

Eugene listened patiently but always courteously explained that God had called him to found a tabernacle in some large American city. This never satisfied Chung. The next time he encountered Eugene, he pursued him with the same fervor.

Finally, in 1929 Dad gave in to Chung's urging and appealed to his Asbury teammates to accompany him on an Asian mission tour. The three men, Byron Crouse, Virgil Kirkpatrick, and Eugene, were designated as the Asbury College Missionary Team. Since the other two men were musical, they urged Eugene to learn to play the trombone. Dad was an excellent pianist and in a surprisingly short time was playing the trombone. Now every meeting featured not only zealous preaching but also a brass trio.

With the onset of the Great Depression that year, it seemed that the three men could not have chosen a worse time to begin a world tour. Sources of money for the anticipated trip had almost dried up. Even President Morrison advised that it might be wise to postpone the tour for a few years until things had settled down economically. Still, they proceeded to Los Angeles where they were scheduled to hold meetings in the large Pasadena Pilgrim Holiness Church pastored by Seth Rees, the founder of the denomination. Unlike other more cautious friends, Rees encouraged the fellows to go ahead as planned. "God will provide and we will stand behind you," he assured them.

Thus encouraged, the team boarded a ship in San Francisco destined for Japan, their first stop. Here they would be the guests of Bud and Hazel Kilbourne. Bud was the son of Ernest Kilbourne, one of the founders of The Oriental Missionary Society (now One Mission Society, known as OMS). The mission president at this time was Lettie Cowman, the well-known author of *Streams in the Desert* and *Missionary Warrior*.

The arrival of the men in Tokyo coincided with the start of the annual conference of the Japan Holiness Church, the third-largest denomination in Japan at that time. Thousands of church members gathered on the campus of the Bible school in the Shinjuku district. The impression that this gathering made on Dad cannot be overestimated. He later said, "When I was in Japan, I definitely felt that God was calling me to be a missionary somewhere in the Orient."

If the Japan convention impressed the trio, three weeks in Korea did even more. Robert Chung met the men in Seoul. He had arranged a full itinerary and served as interpreter for the team and especially for Dad who was the main speaker. Large crowds attended the meetings with many conversions. The team also held special services for the missionary community.

Before the trio left Los Angeles, Mrs. Cowman had taken Dad aside. She knew of his mother's concern that her son find a wife of God's choosing. Lettie, with a sly twinkle in her eye and characteristic prophetic boldness, said to Dad, "Eugene, when you get to China, you are going to meet your Waterloo." At that time, he laughed off her remarks as the influence of his mother's wishful thinking.

The first night in China, the boys stayed with missionaries in Canton. The following morning, as the team and missionaries sat down to breakfast, there appeared on the staircase an attractive young lady who had come to China as a secretary. Her name was Esther Helsby, and her family's home had been a frequent stopping place for the Cowmans and Reeses on their yearly visit to Maryland to speak at the Pilgrim Holiness Church's Denton Camp Meeting.

Prior to the trio's departure from the U.S., Eugene had exacted from his companions promises that they would not allow any female distractions to interfere with their mission. "We must keep our minds on the work to which God has called us," he said. They all agreed.

After meeting Esther at that first breakfast, Eugene decided that perhaps their mission might possibly include an enlarged agenda. Before the men left Canton on a tour to other OMS stations in China, they agreed to join the missionaries at a summer resort in Japan. It took only a few weeks after that before Eugene and Esther were engaged.

The trio continued their tour to other countries, most notably to India. In this environment, Eugene became conscious of what he felt was a divine call to the vast Hindu nation. Following numerous meetings in India, the men traveled to the Middle East and Europe. Altogether they were gone almost a year.

Eugene and Esther were married December 23, 1930, in Milton, Pennsylvania, where Esther's father pastored the Pilgrim Holiness Church, situated on a tributary of the Susquehanna River. The two returned to China as missionaries with OMS the following year. They were stationed in Peking on the Bible school campus.

The property OMS purchased had been the former lavish house of a Chinese prince who ministered in the nearby Forbidden City. So ostentatious was their home that they recall nationals who, upon entering the living room, stood speechless and then carefully tiptoed around the magnificent Peking carpet.

By the time their first son, Robert, was born in 1933, Dad had fallen in love with the huge world of charm and contradictions which was China. In the shadow of palaces of unimaginable splendor lived half-clothed beggars in abject poverty. Dad, along with other missionaries, notably Uri Chandler and Rolland Rice, organized the China Every Creature Crusade, then termed The Great Village Campaign and now known as Every Community for Christ. This was patterned after the Japan crusade, which in 1918 completed the distribution of God's Word to every one of Japan's 10,400,000 homes.

By the time I was born in 1936, Bobbie (Robert) spoke perfect Chinese, far better than either of his parents. Esther, who had her heart set on having a girl, was very disappointed that number two was also a boy. We two boys, close in age, were to entertain her with our constant squabbles and feuding for years to come.

I was just six months old when one night, due to electrical wiring problems, our home caught fire, a fire that hastily spread to the teachers' and students' quarters. Part of our family lore is that the only salvaged possession was a small bundle of my diapers. The Peking fire truck finally arrived but the fire hydrant was dry.

Chinese friends gathered the next day to offer our family not only their condolences but also generous gifts of clothing and other necessities. Forever after, my parents remembered, that tragic day was in fact one of unparalleled blessing. For them, it put to rest the issue of the foreigners' vast material wealth which so often separated the missionaries from the Chinese. With the loss of our home, missionaries and nationals truly seemed like brothers and sisters. My parents never again were tempted to furnish our homes with such ostentatious and "amazingly inexpensive" furnishings.

In 1937, Japan invaded China, inciting the Second Sino-Japanese War. The United States was not yet at war with Japan, so most missionaries elected to continue their work in China, hopeful that somehow hostilities would be resolved.

Our furlough came due in 1938. I was only two, but I retain a few fragmentary memories of that year in the U.S. We spent Christmas and part of the winter with Mother's parents, the Helsbys, in Gloversville, New York, where Grandpa was pastoring.

A tragic reminder of those days was a sad mishap that took place while Dad and Mother were away in meetings and my sibling and I were staying with our grandparents. Bob's accident, which happened while he was endeavoring to untie his shoelaces with a pair of cuticle scissors, resulted in the loss of his left eye. He overcame this handicap in a most remarkable way, becoming both an avid reader and a skillful athlete.

After a brief visit to mission headquarters in Los Angeles, we boarded the SS *President Coolidge* bound for Shanghai. One Mission Society had recently opened a Bible school in the great seaport city and asked Dad to oversee the building of the new campus. Both Mom and Dad taught in the school, and Dad kept busy with itinerant evangelism and church visits.

Bob was old enough to be enrolled in the Shanghai American School. When he returned home that first afternoon and was asked how he liked school, he replied, "It's okay, but I didn't learn it all. I have to go back tomorrow."

CHAPTER 2

INDIA

Japan was decidedly building an Asian empire. It was not difficult to discern her intents. Korea, Manchuria, and Taiwan had already yielded to her military might, and she now viewed them as her colonies. Her next target was all of China.

With much of the Far East closed to missions, OMS leaders were convinced that it would be prudent to establish a new Asian field. The choice was India, which seemed relatively safe as a British colony. The consensus was that Dad was the one to lead the mission into that great sub-continent.

When my parents were informed of this board decision, they were both strongly resistant. After years of Chinese language study, how could they think of transferring to another field? At the same time, Dad could not deny that earlier, on the Asbury trio mission tour, he had a very clear impression that India was in God's plan for their future. As Mother and Dad made this a matter of prayer, they both received a clear word from Scripture that indeed God was calling them to India.

In the fall of 1941, we arrived in India and located in the southern British capital of Bangalore. Other colleagues joined us there. After much prayer and counsel from mission leaders, it was agreed that OMS would have two centers. They would open Bible schools and plant churches in Allahabad in the north and Gadag in the south.

Shortly thereafter came news of the attack on Pearl Harbor on December 7, 1941. All of our missionaries still residing in China were imprisoned by the Japanese in two camps, located in Shanghai and Weihsien. Though India was temporarily safe under British rule and protection, the Japanese army had already started their relentless march through Southeast Asia.

The OMS team was divided and assigned to the two centers. Wesley and Betty Duewel teamed with the Ernys in founding the Allahabad Bible Seminary on an eight-acre property formerly owned by a large British girls' school. It had been deserted and unattended for decades and now appeared almost like a jungle. Later Bob and I would have part of the joy of cutting down the vast tangles of undergrowth, eventually turning the property into something resembling a park.

At this point came the initiation of our family's acquaintance with boarding schools. Since we were in North India, the logical choice was Woodstock, the world's oldest boarding school for missionary children, dating back to the U.S. Civil War. That first year Bob became part of the boarding school society. Since I was still in kindergarten, I studied at home with Mother. The following year both Bob and I were residents of Ridgewood Dormitory, the home for smaller boys at Woodstock.

I remember early pangs of homesickness and feelings of utter desertion upon entering boarding school. This was my first-ever separation from my parents. But soon I found myself content and happy in that close-knit society replete with excellent teachers and harmless gangs of small boys all living in the indescribable beauty of the Himalayas, which boasts the highest peaks in the world. From Landour we could never quite see Mount Everest at 29,000 feet, but on a clear day Bandarpunch (Monkey's Tail) was clearly visible at 20,700 feet.

In the summer, the folks came up to Landour and Woodstock for a couple of months to enjoy a break from the Allahabad heat and all-encompassing dust storms that rolled down the Ganges Valley. When they arrived, we would leave our dorm rooms and reside with them. One Mission Society eventually bought Tipperary, a cottage where missionaries could spend the summer months.

Dad, whose schedule was always full, religiously reserved several weeks in the mountains for picnics, games, and, above all, a hike into the interior. This would mean a very rigorous walk of ten to twenty miles. We were equipped with army surplus backpacks, as well as sleeping bags. If ever there was a paradise created for the delight of young boys, it was this wonderfully wooded landscape and the challenging treks back through the towering peaks and valleys.

Winter vacation, when all Woodstock students returned to their homes on the plains, meant a sudden and altogether different lifestyle for us. The folks were lodged in a huge, castle-like structure of Victorian architecture on the campus of the former British school. With mischievous boys bent on some kind of mild mayhem, no environment could have been more perfect. All of the buildings were joined by adjacent flat roofs, creating a haven for adventures. Inside, ceilings soared to heights of up to twenty feet, built that way on the theory that, since heat rises, the higher the ceiling, the cooler the room.

Our constant companions during those winter vacation months were the Khanna boys, Chandra and Sundar, sons of Pastor Gobichand Khanna, Dad's associate. Pastor Khanna's rotund and lovable wife was a lady of remarkable good temper in light of the mischief we hatched. The Khanna and Erny boys formed a sort of Tom Sawyer-like association.

One of our treks took us to the banks of the Ganges River, full of crocodiles and corpses bound in decaying muslin, some floating close to the surface. Membership in our gang required that all of us drink a bottle of water from the river. Drinking this libation from the holy Ganges was incredibly foolish, since this sacred river was the repository of the bodies of people who had died of every conceivable disease.

With most afternoons and weekends free, we found adventures that would have thrilled the most daring. On one of our jaunts we chanced upon two human skulls lying side by side and bleached a brilliant white in the sands of the Ganges. One of us suggested that we keep them as souvenirs. Returning to the campus we decided to employ these lovely oval delights as soccer balls. We chose teams and presently were kicking our rare treasures of human remains across the seminary grounds.

The Duewel bungalow was situated close to our impromptu goal. Looking out his study window, Uncle Wesley, principal of the Bible school, saw our impious shenanigans. In an instant, he rushed out the front door and advanced toward us with upraised hands, crying, "Boys! Boys!" Mystified that our soccer game would be so rudely interrupted and had provoked such an outcry, we brought the game to a halt. Quietly now, Wesley explained to us the possible consequences of defiling human remains in this land of infinite superstition and fears related to one's afterlife. We never found out what Uncle Wesley did with those human heads, and we never dared ask.

We played a variety of native games, and one Christmas all four of us boys received gifts of field hockey sticks. We soon discovered what an effective weapon those heavy sticks could be!

But all was not fun and games. Mother and Dad fell victim to some of the common diseases of that climate, especially malaria and amoebic dysentery, in perpetuity. Without the wonder drugs of later years, sulfa could only do so much. Dad began to lose weight, eventually a full eighty pounds, turning into a skeletal shadow of his former vigorous self. Mother began for the first time in her life to experience depression of a most fearful sort, a malady she suffered off and on until her passing at age eighty-nine.

While on vacation one time in Allahabad, during family prayers, my parents asked me if I would like to accept Christ into my heart. I definitely realized that I needed forgiveness and a Savior. After praying to receive Jesus, there came a wonderful peace and change of heart. As I crawled under the mosquito net into my bed that night, I told my brother, Bob, that I loved him.

During one vacation Bob and I joined the vast crowds at the great melee, where every year millions of pious Hindus bathe in the holy Ganges and Jumna rivers to wash away their sins. We were in the company of our Bible school students helping to distribute tracts.

Afterwards I came down with the terrifying disease of infantile paralysis, or polio. I was eight years old, and the Salk vaccine was still unknown. The best Dr. Berar, the lone American doctor in town, could advise was the still-unproven Sister Kenny treatment. This consisted of around-the-clock applications of hot packs soaked in scalding water and immediately applied to my back and legs and other areas affected by the disease. Minister friends came and laid hands on me, praying for my healing.

Gradually I began to improve and, though I was not permitted to leave on schedule for boarding school that March, by April I was well, healthy, active, and back at Woodstock in second standard, the U.S. equivalent of third grade. My teacher was a Miss Ahrens, a stern Anglo-Indian woman, who not only taught during the day but was also dorm matron at Ridgewood in the evening. She had a fearful temper, but her redeeming factor was the skill she had of telling ghost stories after we were in bed, and after long shadows enveloped the Ridgewood domain. What a gift she had for infusing sheer terror into the hearts of young boys.

When we returned to school each March, our party was

made up of Woodstock students in the Allahabad area. We met at the EIR (East India Railroad) station. The trains never left on schedule, but in time we would all be ensconced with an adult chaperone in one of the carriages headed for Dehradun, the terminus of the rail line, where we boarded a rickety bus and began the ascent to Mussoorie, situated six thousand feet up in the foothills of the Himalayas. The precipitous ride finally deposited us near Landour, where Woodstock was located.

Most Woodstock students were missionary kids, mainly of Western descent. The student body consisted of an intriguing mix of Methodists, Presbyterians, Pentecostals, and Episcopalians. Sad to say, however, religion was for the most part viewed more as a sort of cultural necessity than as any personal experience. Still, attending church and chapel was required, and our behavior was remarkably wholesome and virtuous. There were also English-speaking Asian classmates of various faiths: Hindus, Muslims, Sikhs, Parsees, and atheists.

Some of these students were scions of India's wealthiest families. Two of my best friends were boys from giant industrial company families. In these years prior to independence, there were princes and princesses at Woodstock who were heirs to India's fabulously rich city-states. After independence, these areas were permitted autonomy but with the proviso that the monarchs submit in all things to the central government.

In this curious mix of races and peoples, there developed a unique society with its own practices and language, a sort of patois of English and Hindustani and a smattering of Urdu, intelligible only to denizens of Woodstock students. Older boys were called *hefts* and younger ones *chuts*. Girls were always *dames*, and things that one regarded as satisfactory were called *pukka*. If anything was excellent beyond being *pukka*, it was designated *pukka ding chaunce*. Smaller boys would innocently refer to their older brothers as *my bra*, having at that time never heard that word applied to a female undergarment. On and on went our list of perversions of the human language.

With the outbreak of World War II, any notions my parents had of a new addition to our family were put on hold. Yet in 1943, when Mother discovered she was expecting, they joyfully viewed the event as a divine intervention. With two hyperactive and frequently troublesome sons, Mother longed for a girl.

Her prayers were answered that August when our sister put in her appearance. She was cute, adorable, and had curly blond hair which Mom soon fashioned into Shirley Temple ringlets. Mother, an admirer of Evangeline Booth (daughter of William Booth, the founder of The Salvation Army), gave her daughter that same noble name which was soon abbreviated to Vangie. Without a doubt, the presence of a charming little female in the house did much to offset the crude and hostile antics of her brothers.

After the war, for our second furlough in 1946, we waited in Calcutta for a month to board the crowded USNS *Marine Lynx*, a troop carrier now being used to ferry civilians across the Pacific with stops in Shanghai, Hong Kong, and Tokyo, altogether a six-week voyage. The sexes were segregated, so Dad and Bob and I slept five decks below where bunks were stacked three or four high. This created difficulty when needing the toilet at night and even more so when suffering a sudden attack of seasickness. It was autumn and the ocean was rough. In our lower bunkroom dungeon, when the vessel pitched, novice sailors were at first all susceptible to perpetual seasickness. Our Asian passengers, particularly the Chinese, seemed even more inclined to the heaves.

Mother and Vangie, who was now covered with splotches of red due to an infected rash that had broken out as a result of prickly heat in Calcutta, lodged with other women and small children in a stateroom located on a deck far closer to sea level.

This voyage afforded Bob and me our first taste of American soda pop. Disappointingly, however, the ship was apparently stocked with Pepsi-Cola, not the all-American drink synonymous with Uncle Sam and Old Glory – Coca-Cola. This seemed a cruel trick to play on boys who had waited virtually all their lives for a swig of that Yankee nectar, Coke. Sometime later in the voyage, however, they broke out the Coca-Cola and, to our surprise, we discovered that we liked Pepsi better, probably because the sixteen-ounce bottles were more of a bargain than the tiny six-ounce figure-shaped Coke containers. Best of all, we found out that empty pop bottles were of inestimable value. A refund netted a penny each and sometimes two. Bob and I promptly went into business and soon had a pot full of American coins.

For this 1946-48 furlough, the mission decided that we should live in Winona Lake, Indiana, which was situated in the heart of the OMS constituency. Winona Lake was famed for its great summer conferences begun by Billy Sunday who had built the huge ten-thousand-seat tabernacle. I attended the local elementary school. The fifth grade teacher endeared herself to us by reading the *Sugar Creek Gang* series. Bob traveled by bus to Warsaw High School where he learned how painful and difficult it was for newcomers to find friends and acceptance in an American high school.

When winter came, we bought sleds and caromed down the midtown steep incline that the town youngsters knew so well. Summers in this lakeside village offered the joys of boating and water fun. Here I learned to swim.

Following the war, automobiles, even older ones, were practically impossible to come by. Uncle Bill Erny, who still headed the family business, provided us with a used Ford but soon replaced it with a brand new shiny black Nash.

Dad was continually in demand as a church and conference

speaker. Mother was left most of the year in the old rented cottage, the walls a depressing gray, where she had to put up with an ancient coal furnace. With Dad, the referee, away, the perpetual feuds between Bob and me reached unprecedented levels. Vangie's sweet disposition was Mother's lone succor.

Young children's early joys leave indelible impressions. That year I was introduced to comic books (my favorite was *Captain Marvel*) and a Red Ryder BB gun, the very model coveted by the boy in *A Christmas Story*.

Shortly after returning to India from furlough, we received word that Dad had been elected OMS president. This was 1949, the same year that Bob graduated from high school. The prospect of leaving our dear school and community came to me as something of a shock, if not a tragedy. Parting with my Woodstock friends before graduation was unthinkable. A somber and premature farewell cast across my life a sort of gloom, especially the prospect of parting with Alex Thomson, my dearest friend, whose mother served with the Ceylon and India General Mission.

Mom, Dad, and Vangie came up the mountain for Bob's graduation. After that, we took a tour of some of India's most famous sights, including the Taj Mahal. Then back in Allahabad there was a seminary, church, and mission farewell which included gifts and a long poem lamenting the darkening of the sun and the cessation of bird songs!

For the first time, we returned to the homeland not only by ship, but also by air. We were scheduled to fly to Hong Kong and from there complete the journey by boat aboard the SS *General W.H. Gordon*.

That family flight occupies a place unprecedented in the family archives. Pan American flew without incident over the Himalayas to Hong Kong, but in order to land in the great port city, the plane was required to negotiate an exceedingly narrow runway carved out of the low mountains that surround the Hong Kong harbor. The terror of this landing was exacerbated by several factors. Not only was the runway very narrow, it was also shrouded with fog. Our carrier repeatedly encountered what is known as air pockets which caused the plane to drop hundreds of feet straight down as though on a malfunctioning elevator, and very much like the first sensation of riding a roller coaster. Luggage stashed in unenclosed shelves above our heads frequently dislodged and fell directly on us.

Upon these sudden descents, Mother could not suppress the sharp inhaling of terrified gasps and even small screams. When we finally landed, there came audible prayers of thanks and her inward resolution to never fly again. Following the voyage to San Francisco, we were met by our Erny relatives, two families of which were now residing in California. Our chauffeur was Claude Young, the Methodist minister who had married Dad's sister Jeanette.

Thus, after so brief a period of time, I was severed from the comfortable, familiar Woodstock environment and plunged into a world that loomed before me as a terrifying unknown.

CHAPTER 3

A NEW ENVIRONMENT

After moving to the U.S., every summer we found ourselves returning to Winona Lake, Indiana, for the week-long OMS International Convention. The services always ended on a Sunday afternoon and usually featured the dynamic Bob Pierce, who could hold an audience spellbound for two hours or more. After the devastation of the Korean War, Bob, along with Elmer Kilbourne, was instrumental in founding, supporting, and heading up World Vision, which ministered to the needs of many left as orphans and widows.

Summers following the convention were mostly spent with Mother's parents, the Helsbys, now living on the eastern shore of Maryland, not far from Chesapeake Bay.

Dad's parents had both died during the 1930s, and I have no memory of either of them, but those summer days with Grandpa and Grandma Helsby in Maryland remain as some of my richest childhood memories.

Grandpa, Lindley Helsby, grew up on a farm along the narrow peninsula that is the eastern shore of Maryland. He had little education and no prospects other than to farm as his father and ancestors had done. As a teen, however, he and two of his friends were tremendously impacted by a revival held one summer in that part of the state. The three of them were soundly converted, and two of them were called to preach. Lindley enrolled in God's Bible School and College in Cincinnati to prepare for the ministry.

By 1949, Grandpa was nearing retirement. As a Pilgrim Holiness pastor, he received no regular retirement assistance. Early every summer, however, he put in a large and impressive garden, featuring tomatoes, sweet corn, and lima beans. Best of all, in my thinking, Grandpa loved to fish, and the eastern shore of Maryland was a fisherman's paradise. A preacher friend had a good-sized boat and took us out for wonderful hours on the water, employing hand lines to fish off the bottom.

On occasion, Dad went along on these fishing trips, not because he had any interest in fishing but because he regarded this as his fatherly responsibility. He was textbook choleric, and everyone knew he regarded fishing as a pointless waste of good time. His mind was always stirring with fresh schemes and strategies for enlarging The Oriental Missionary Society and building churches in Asia and South America. Once in a while, when the fish were biting furiously, he admitted that it did afford some degree of pleasure. For the most part, however, his demeanor powerfully conveyed the fact that he would feel far better employed in kingdom ventures.

When I wasn't fishing, I enjoyed shooting my BB gun. With a little luck, I could pick off a starling from the flock that loved to occupy the upper branches of the big oak tree beside the Helsby home.

One of Mother's relatives, Charles Adams, owned a cannery. He hired me to pick tomatoes, the hardest physical work that I had ever done. This meant bending over in a stooped position hour after hour, plucking the ripe tomatoes and placing them in baskets that, when filled, weighed about thirty pounds. This was hard enough, but what followed was worse: lifting the burdensome baskets into a huge semi. At the time, I was thirteen and skinny as a rail. A few hours of this onerous chore convinced me that tomato picking and loading was not my calling in life.

The other memorable task assigned to me by Grandpa Helsby was emptying the parsonage cesspool situated in the backyard just next to the rows of beans. For pecuniary reasons, the idea of employing a professional for this task never entered Grandpa's mind.

As we bailed out the nauseating sewage by hand, it soon became impossible to reach the deeper contents without physically lowering someone into the cesspool. Grandpa suggested that since I was small enough to fit through the narrow opening, I should descend bodily into the septic tank. For this, he provided me with hip boots. Laboriously I filled bucket after bucket of the unmentionable contents and raised it dripping above my head and up through the narrow opening. The filled bucket was almost too heavy for me, and I managed to splatter the contents over myself as I raised it to his waiting hand. When the task was done, Grandpa gave me a wry smile and said, "Well, you really earned your supper tonight."

My high school years were, to a large degree, shielded from the dominating California influence. For this I owe a debt beyond calculation to Culter Academy, a small Christian school at Third and Westmoreland, founded by Mabel Culter, who had been a missionary to Korea. She had followed God's call to open, by faith and at great personal sacrifice, a truly Christian school in the heart of Los Angeles.

Leaving India when Dad was elected president of the mission, we moved to Los Angeles, actually Hollywood, where OMS had its headquarters. That fall I was enrolled in Culter as a sophomore, straight from Woodstock and the Himalayas. I was terrified. From the comfortable world of half-civilized boarding school culture, I was now plunged unceremoniously into the changing world of post-World War II California. No culture shock could have been greater.

This resulted in my first experience with depression. I knew no one in the small high school and was now clearly the object of some curiosity. I particularly remember that first day of school. My haircut was no longer in fashion, and I arrived wearing a pastor's old suit coat and sought all day for a place to hang the humiliating garment. But since I was too shy to inquire as to the location of the cloakroom, I carried that coat draped over my arm from class to class, even to P.E., and back to the street corner where I caught the bus home. Out of the peculiar agonies of this phase of my life, I learned all too well what it means to be "a fish out of water."

Two things gradually came to my rescue in these painful days. In P.E. I drew some admiration from classmates when it was discovered that I was the fastest runner in the class and the best jumper. The previous year on the Woodstock basketball court, I had developed a spectacular hook shot which was still in working order when I took my classmates on in games of "horse."

The second surprising success came in the form of a lissome classmate who lived just a block down from us on North Hobart Boulevard. Carol Haines was also an MK (missionary kid) and was recently home from Colombia, South America, where her parents had worked with OMS. Long waits at the bus stop on Melrose each weekday provided a welcome opportunity to nurture our timid friendship, a friendship that eventually delivered delightful dividends. Soon, Carol and I were dating.

Of all the Divine Providence that God showered upon my young life, none, I believe, was more significant than my three years at Culter Academy. The institution never flourished financially, but with the help of a friend and patron, Mrs. Kerr, of the famous Kerr Mason Jar Company, it was possible to relocate

Culter on the campus of a school once attended by Shirley Temple. Time, however, had not been kind to the property. By the early 1950s, the once-beautiful swimming pool was a wreck and totally unusable. The main buildings, designed like a Swiss chalet, had been condemned by the Los Angeles fire department, and it took some effort and a lot of funding before the property could meet the demands of the city's building code.

The large playground and sports field, for the most part, resembled a cow pasture. The school had no proper basketball court. Thus, for serious practices and games, we had to hitchhike miles south on Western Avenue to the Roger Williams Baptist Church, which generously allowed us the use of their facility.

I had inherited some of Dad's athletic abilities and by my senior year had my name on most of the major Culter trophies, with the exception of baseball. When it came to our national pastime, I was at a lamentable disadvantage. This was due to the fact that during my early school years at Woodstock, which was situated in the mountains, it was virtually impossible to carve out of the steep hillsides any field large enough for baseball, a sport in which the little ball is driven as far as four hundred feet from home base.

I contend, however, that despite the limited accoutrements of the institution, no finer Christian school ever existed. The underpaid faculty loved the school and ministered to us with genuine affection and a happy, sanctified spirit that I had found only on primitive mission fields. Their presence in the unadorned classrooms was a kind of sacrament. A number of those teachers were part of a local Plymouth Brethren fellowship. No teachers knew the Bible as well as Marchand King, Pamela Reeve, and the school's founder, Miss Culter.

Occasionally Bible classes were taught by leaders in the new Navigators' organization, founded by Dawson Trotman and located in Pasadena, which was some distance from the school. The zealous Navs got us all memorizing Scripture. Our weekly assignments included memorizing three Bible verses. Dave Broughm, our football coach, had played football for Washington State and inspired in me a passion for football. Today I look back on that Culter period with profound gratitude. Our class of 1953, until then the largest class ever, celebrated our fiftieth anniversary in 2003. The reunion was held at a Bible conference facility near San Diego. Few in the class are not vibrant, born-again Christians, and many among them are homeland and overseas ministers and missionaries.

CHAPTER 4

YOSEMITE

Following graduation from high school, it was important that I work summers to pay for college tuition for the coming year. No assistance would be forthcoming from my parents or any living relative. Dad told us we should be grateful for the fifty dollars a month that the mission provided to help MKs through college.

Some years earlier our cousins, the Householders and Youngs, had discovered that without question the best place to find summer work was in California's famed Yosemite National Park. By the time I graduated from high school, Bob, who had already begun working at Yosemite's Camp Curry, urged me to join him.

Since his college began its summer vacation a couple of weeks earlier than my high school did, he went ahead to the park with friends, leaving me to drive his '38 Plymouth up the mountain. At just seventeen years old, I had only been driving a few months and never any great distance. Now with trembling, I set out on my very first solo drive over an unfamiliar road up to an unknown place where I was to apply for an uncertain job.

I started out long before daybreak, and by the time the sun rose, I found myself on the steep "grapevine" incline, famous for boiling radiators and assorted engine problems. This notorious grade leads out of the Los Angeles basin and into the San

Fernando Valley, author John Steinbeck country. In those days without a cell phone or credit card and only a few dollars in my pocket, traveling in Bob's antiquated Plymouth filled me with assorted frightful scenarios. You can be sure I was praying fervently all the way.

This was the start of a lifelong love affair. Above Fresno, within a relatively small valley, I discovered some of the most beautiful scenery in the world.

There are only two occasions apart from my first roller coaster ride that have literally left me breathless. One was my first sight of the Grand Canyon, which I later regularly passed on my annual pilgrimage from California to Kentucky. The other was my first view of Yosemite Valley. I had heard my cousins raving about the park with the unpronounceable name. I wondered what it was about this place that provoked such excited and endless comment. Driving in through the west gate, I passed the famous big trees, some so huge you can actually drive a car through the tunnel hewn in a tree's trunk. The next twenty miles consist of pleasant park scenery, wooded slopes covered with pine trees and carpeted with needles.

As I approached the Wawona Tunnel, there is no hint of anything other than a commonplace passageway carved out of another ordinary mountain. Emerging into the daylight, however, I confronted my second-most awesome sight. There it was, a panorama nearly without parallel. Called "the valley of hanging rivers," I saw two beautiful waterfalls. From great heights, cataracts of water were plunging down granite walls into the Merced River, the ancient waterway credited with carving out Yosemite Valley.

To my left there appeared the world's largest piece of exposed granite, El Capitan, four times the size of the Rock of Gibraltar. It presented a huge sunlit wall soaring straight up from the valley floor for three-quarters of a mile. Climbing El Capitan is the supreme challenge for the world's greatest mountaineers and rock climbers.

Driving on a distance, I approached Yosemite Falls, which locals call the world's highest waterfall, higher than Angel Falls in Brazil. This honor, however, requires verbal agility. What appears as a single waterfall from a distance, upon closer examination turns out to be two waterfalls, the Upper Yosemite Falls and the Lower. In the spring and early summer with the snow melting, the falls are full, beautifully shaped, and of exquisite elongated beauty. Passing the appropriately named Bridal Veil Falls, on the right is soaring Glacier Point, a shaft of gray rock that veers heavenward at a dizzying angle.

At the base of Glacier Point is Camp Curry, named for the wealthy San Francisco family that early on developed Yosemite Valley and was rewarded with a prized governmental concession – the solitary management of the park. Part of Camp Curry consists of tent villages for employees. These tents were destined to be my summer home for the next four years.

From the meadow and Curry parking lot, one encounters what is often called the world's most photographed mountain, Half Dome. Eons ago, we are informed, during the great ice age, a massive glacier moved through the Sierras shearing the vast granite mountain cleanly in half and creating Yosemite Valley. Local lore tells of a hiker in the park, driven by compulsions we can only imagine, who leaped off the face of Half Dome to his death. Rangers found his backpack on the crest of the mountain and a note saying simply, "I always wanted the world's largest tombstone."

A brief but steep walk through Camp Curry to the other end of Yosemite Valley brings within view two more spectacular falls: first, Vernal, and then straight above, Nevada. That so many spectacular natural wonders should be fitted into so small an area is part of the miracle of Yosemite, for the valley itself occupies no more than a few square miles. The entire park, however, is one of America's largest, occupying an area as large as the state of Rhode Island.

In the upper reaches of the Sierras are towering pines and blissful valleys, at the base of which the melting snows have created hundreds of lakes. Employees who had the same day off often formed hiking clubs. Bob and I and our companions hiked gleefully over the spectacular peaks and valleys in what is known as the high country. Here and there are small tent villages with exotic names. These are for the convenience of any who are adventurous enough to climb the scores of steep mountain trails.

For our favorite hike, we would drive to the high country and leave the car in the Tuolumne parking lot at Lake Tenaya at the foot of three imposing heaps of rock dubbed the Ragged Peaks. Meandering down along the miles of rivers formed by the melting snow, one comes to Glen Aulin, Vogelsang, and Merced Lake, the most famous of the upper Sierra camps.

It is a seven-mile trail from Tuolumne Meadows and Soda Springs to our favorite destination, Glen Aulin. One summer when I was in particularly good shape (the result of walking many miles a day in the Curry dining room, called the largest dining room west of the Mississippi), I ran the entire seven miles, mostly uphill, from Glen Aulin to the Tuolumne parking lot. In my late teens I had what I felt was boundless energy. From my present perspective, at seventy-seven years old and hampered by an artificial hip, I look back upon those youthful exploits with a kind of awe and wonder.

That first summer I anticipated working at Camp Curry with Bob, who had informed me that there was an urgent need for another dishwasher in the dining room kitchen. This was his third summer in the huge restaurant, and he assured me that a brief word to the chef, Mr. Rasmussen, would land me the job. Bob had graduated from dishwasher to pot-washer and then waiter, a coveted position. The kitchen employees made a decent wage, but it was the waiters who got tips and free meals.

Chef Rasmussen was agreeable enough to my working in his dining room until he asked, "How old are you, son? You need to be at least eighteen to work in food services." Due to a difference in the school year schedules, I skipped a year when I transferred from Woodstock in India to Culter Academy in Los Angeles. I graduated from high school six weeks after my seventeenth birthday.

"I am seventeen," I told the chef.

"No problem," he responded. "Just write eighteen on your application form." This was no problem for Rasmussen but a huge problem for me. I had been taught never to lie and was not about to begin breaking one of God's commandments my first summer away from home.

At the Yosemite Park and Curry Company office (YPCC) that afternoon, I dutifully entered my age as seventeen. The chef was right. My youthfulness ruled out the possibility of any work in food services. I was offered a job, not in Camp Curry near my brother, but at the opposite side of the valley in a housing area known simply as The Lodge.

There I would be starting at the very bottom of the company wage scale, ninety cents an hour. No meals. It was all but impossible to save any summer earnings. Restaurants in the park had inflated tourists' rates, and the cost of meals alone was soon eating up what little salary I made.

Determined to save, I put myself on a budget calculated to save one-half of all I earned. I soon learned that the cheapest items in the park grocery store were beans or macaroni and cheese. When I did splurge with a meal at The Lodge cafeteria, I'm ashamed to admit that if the diners left a roll or a tasty bear claw on their plates, I was not above pocketing the prize on my way out the door to supplement my next meal. After all, leftover food was destined for the garbage can. I had a far better place to put it.

At the Valley Church youth gatherings that Bob and I attended regularly, I consumed everything I could get my hands on and one evening made myself sick on an overdose of s'mores.

I started at the absolute lowest job in the park, a houseman. I spent my days roaming the housing areas and parking lots picking up bits of trash. Using a long stick equipped with a nail protruding from the bottom, I speared cigarette butts, gum wrappers, and crumpled Camel and Lucky Strike packages. These were deposited in a bag, which I hung over my shoulder. Frequently, tourists observing my lowly toil smiled and remarked, "I see that business is still picking up." How I hated that job. Time never passed more slowly. An hour seemed a small eternity and eight hours a miserable and endless period of time. Unlike most park employees, this job provided me no companionship, no fellow employees to chat with as I trudged along over the grounds at the lowliest task in all the valley.

Lodge employees were housed in various tent areas. My assigned tent was a good distance from Camp Curry where Bob worked. Now, not only was I not working near Bob, I also hardly ever saw him. And since my job was a mile or more from my sleeping quarters, I was left with a transportation problem. Bob, sympathetic and generous, let me use his trusty '38 Plymouth to go back and forth, a favor for which I was exceedingly grateful, especially the next week when I met Marianne.

It was early June, the proverbial month celebrated by James Russell Lowell with "What is so rare as a day in June, then, if ever, come perfect days." Here I was, in what is doubtless the most beautiful valley in the entire earth, too young to get a decent job, but ready for some female companionship.

That week, picking up trash along the paths and reduced

to the bottom rung of the employee ladder, I prayed for some kind of consolation. God heard my prayer. She stood before me that spring morning, sunlight filtering through the pines, turning her yellow hair into a halo. "Hi," she ventured, flashing me an enchanting smile containing far more, I imagined, than any mere greeting. Even her name, Marianne, had about it the tinkle of a bell.

She was not the least bit shy. "Could I see you later?" she asked. "Maybe we could get together after work."

"Yah, that would be nice," I mumbled. My eyes were glazed, a warm core of emotion rising somewhere within me.

After Carol, my steady during my sophomore and junior years at Culter, I had begun dating Margi Blackstone. She was the charming and talented daughter of Reverend Blackstone, an associate pastor of the famous Hollywood First Presbyterian Church. Her parents had formerly been missionaries to China so we had something in common.

By graduation that summer, I viewed Margi as my girlfriend. In Yosemite, I started up a hopeful correspondence with her but unfortunately seldom received a response. Then I heard from friends informing me that my idea of going steady and Margi's were quite different. She was frequently seen in the company of handsome young men of which there was no shortage in Hollywood Pres, a popular church, where a good number of movie stars worshiped.

That evening I picked up Marianne at her dorm and we drove in Bob's Plymouth to the Awani Hotel, the luxurious establishment where I could not afford even a snack. Its location was perfect for a summer romance. From the porch, looking to the right, one saw the towering Yosemite Falls. Straight ahead and three thousand feet straight up was the dizzying rock face of Glacier Point, from which at eight o'clock sharp each night the unforgettable Firefall cascaded. That evening with Marianne was for my young mind a perfect drama, literally a delightful gift from God.

My brother Bob encountered the same phenomenon. His first summer, it had been Joan and the next summer, Pat. Then, after he married Phyllis in 1954, that summer they walked those same Yosemite trails, dreamy-eyed and contented.

Marianne came from northern California, the greater San Francisco area, and was heading that fall to the University of California at Berkeley. Her family was outstanding and accomplished, church people of a sort, whose father she informed me was governed by the wise counsel of "moderation in all things." I informed her that in matters of religious faith, passion and zeal – not moderation – were to be the norm. I also schooled her in the evils of dancing, an appalling idea to her.

With the luxury of Bob's automobile, we enjoyed many romantic evenings. One night, on an impulse, we climbed the steep trail that snakes its way to the top of Yosemite Falls. I am very grateful that in our missionary home, we had been well versed in the necessity of proper and sanctified conduct in all things. As a result, I can look back on that time with Marianne with no regrets.

I discussed my faith with Marianne and gave her the gift of the recently published J.B. Phillips New Testament. She tried to read it, she told me later, but found it insufferably dull. At summer's end, I told her of a popular church in Berkeley pastored by the well-known evangelical Robert Boyd Munger, author of the booklet *My Heart-Christ's Home*. When we parted at summer's end, Marianne wrote to me faithfully for a while. Early on, I received her letter telling me with great joy that she had attended a college retreat sponsored by Pastor Munger's church. There she had received Christ as Savior. As time went on, we occasionally kept in contact. She eventually informed me that, after marriage, she and her husband served in South America as missionaries.

My friendship with Marianne was followed by other romances. After my sojourn at The Lodge as a lowly houseman, the next summer I turned eighteen and was admitted to the huge Curry dining room where Bob worked. I started there as a busboy, but after the resignation of a number of waiters, I was promoted to that enviable job. Now with my exalted position, I inherited a busgirl, a most attractive blond with the enchanting name of Saundra.

Saundra was from the Oakland area and had a surprisingly shy and gentle nature. She had exceedingly high moral standards, and her dates had counted themselves fortunate to even hold her hand. There was a certain sad quality about Saundra, however. I learned that she came from a difficult home background. Before the summer ended, she had given her heart to Christ. Back at Asbury, I received her photo and a letter that read: "I remember you saying that I often looked sad. I was sad. Now it's wonderful how I've changed since I received Jesus. My friends all comment on how happy I look."

Lois was my busgirl the following summer, and we became good friends. Small and wiry, she could out-hike almost anyone. She had Mormon friends in Arizona and had become a Mormon, although she understood practically nothing of the church's doctrine. What fun we had hiking the trails to some of Yosemite's highest peaks and sliding down the snowfields that clung to the slopes until late summer. I read poetry to her from my red volume of Palgrave's poems. I also drew her cartoons and, at every chance, talked to her of my faith in Jesus. Before the year was over, she had written, saying she had received Christ, left Mormonism, and was attending a Baptist church.

I've often remembered those summer friendships. Thank

God for the wisdom to keep those relationships pure and my witness bold.

Three of the four summers I worked in the Curry dining room under the command of Chef Rasmussen whom employees often likened to Napoleon. He compensated for his diminutive stature by wearing a towering chef's hat. He possessed fierce eyes and a huge protruding lower lip. His face was created, I thought, for the pleasure of cartoonists. On the back of our beautiful Ansel Adams photo menus, I drew scores of caricatures of the chef. He took it all as a compliment and frequently purloined my work and carried it home, presumably to show his wife. Though he never evidenced any religious sentiment, he took pleasure in allowing three of us, Bob, Jim, and me, to take off Sunday mornings to attend Valley Church.

That picturesque little brown church situated in Yosemite Village also served as the venue for the Valley Singers. "Songs were made to sing while we're young. Every day is spring while we're young." This was a chorus we learned when we joined the singing group. On Thursday evenings, all who had any interest in choral singing gathered to practice for the end-of-the-summer concert. Our favorites were the Rodgers and Hammerstein musicals, especially *Carousel* and *Oklahoma!* Another favorite was *Finian's Rainbow*. This one, I think, was Bob's favorite. On occasion, with a wicked gleam in his eye, he would burst out with "When I'm not near the girl I love, I love the girl I'm near." This provoked interesting responses from OMS friends and, of course, our parents.

I had planned to work in Yosemite again in the summer of 1958, but our heavenly Father intervened, and I was never again employed in that delightful valley. I had hoped that by the final summer of college I would be married and enjoying the bliss of newlyweds while working in an incredibly beautiful environment. But that spring, the hand of God redirected my life in ways that I never could have imagined.

Upon graduation from high school in 1953, my parents could sense that at seventeen I was still too young to venture from home to Asbury College in faraway Kentucky where Bob was now studying. So I enrolled in Pasadena Nazarene College, made famous at that time by Bob Hopkins, one of the best basketball players in America. Not only had he taken the college team to the NAIA finals, but he was also being recruited by the Lakers. Since Hopkins was also a gifted high jumper on the college track team and my specialty was the long jump, we became friends. That first year, when I was just out of high school, I set the college long-jump record of 22 feet, 5½ inches.

That freshman year I resided in the old East Dorm, which was situated next door to the recently constructed library and basketball court, one of the finest in southern California. The floor itself had been placed atop a great bed of springs, a recent innovation. It had become a kind of shrine for devotees at Saturday night contests, where thousands gathered to admire the exploits of Hopkins who, at the time, was averaging more than thirty points per game.

Being a shy newcomer and not a member of the Nazarenes was something of a barrier in making close friendships at Pasadena Nazarene. My year there left me with a mixed bag of memories, including the unforgettable experience of owning my first car.

I had acquired an inglorious and palsied 1929 Model A for seventy-five dollars from my Culter classmate and best friend, Dick Browning. Now that I had transportation, I had an agreement with OMS that every week I would return from college to spend an afternoon caring for the lawns of both the mission office and the residences. The top speed in my old jalopy was forty-five miles per hour. No one had to remind me not to drive too fast.

No company would insure my old jalopy. Not only did it rumble and squeak and vibrate as though it were in its final throes, it also leaked oil so badly I had to be very careful where I parked. Lee Jeffries, OMS business manager, helped me obtain at almost no cost used oil from a nearby Shell station. When a year later I moved east to Kentucky, I faced the dilemma of disposing of my Model A. No one would buy it or repair the notorious leak that left puddles of oil in front of our house. I finally found a junkyard that gave me ten dollars to take it off my hands.

CHAPTER 5

ROUTE 66 TO ASBURY COLLEGE

Asbury College is a long drive from Los Angeles. In the 1950s, with gas selling at the incredibly low price of nineteen cents a gallon, driving was incomparably cheaper than flying. And, if the car was loaded with five or six passengers all sharing expenses, the cost of the trip per student was a bargain indeed.

In those days, it was common for people planning to drive from the West Coast to the East Coast to advertise for passengers in local newspapers. And in the process we met some unforgettable characters, often blue-collar workers. Well-heeled travelers preferred not to travel an interminable forty-eight hours to Kentucky non-stop, except for gas or a bite to eat. None of us could afford either the time or money for overnights in motels on the journey.

These journeys took place before interstates were common across the U.S., and we kept to the famous Route 66. This highway took us to St. Louis, where we would change routes for Lexington, Kentucky, and Asbury College. Traveling four times a year for both summer break and Christmas holidays left Bob and me with some memorable pilgrimages.

My first ride was with a man of questionable character. He never divulged what he did for a living. He was headed for Paoli, Indiana, in a '49 Ford, one of those truly unreliable vehicles fashioned too quickly on assembly lines to meet the urgent demands for transportation after the war. Everyone knew that '49 Fords were still suffering from Ford's post-war retooling. Almost all of them, as I recall, were lemons.

Leaving Los Angeles, we would drive across the Mohave Desert where temperatures commonly reached 115 to 120 degrees. On one such trip, I remember, the owner of the car, an old Chevy, insisted on doing all the driving himself. The man had a heavy foot. I had never before traveled any distance averaging a full ninety miles per hour. What we soon learned in the process was that the car's tires were desperately in need of balancing. We stopped at a gas station in Needles, a blazing outpost near the California and Arizona border. It was the middle of the night, but we found a mechanic on duty who balanced the wheels. Off again over the scorching desert stretches of Arizona and New Mexico, we reached speeds approaching 100 miles per hour.

One driver we rode with was a very zealous middle-aged Pentecostal woman of the Four-Square-Amy-McPherson persuasion. All the way east, she expounded the wondrous powers of a small child evangelist named Marjo, a name devised by uniting the names of Christ's parents. Later Marjo acquired some notoriety and confessed that for all his preaching skills he had no personal faith.

One year we traveled in Bob's '38 Plymouth, which he had purchased from a retired woman in Pasadena. Incredibly, after fifteen years, it had less than twenty thousand miles on it and was a real steal. On the trip, however, the car began to heat up, and soon clouds of steam were issuing from the radiator. The only utensil Bob had suitable for scooping water from a roadside ditch was a six-ounce Coke bottle. It was no small chore to fill that bottle scores of times until he had topped off the radiator.

Most memorable was 1957, my first year in seminary. At Christmas break, I obtained a practically new Cadillac from a dealership in Detroit and agreed to drive the fishtailed Caddy cross-country to an agency in Los Angeles. My only expense was fuel, and by charging my passengers a small fee, the trip was, for me, almost free of charge. Along with my friend Al Vomsteeg, a seminarian, my passengers were the attractive and winsome Gillam girls, Judy and Linda. Their parents had helped to pioneer the OMS mission work in Colombia, South America.

It was a delightful trip all the way to Texas with Judy entertaining us with Spanish jokes. She taught us that the word *bubble gum* in Spanish has a far more interesting and appropriate sound – *Chicle-de-boomba*!

An hour out of Sweetwater, we ran into an early snow. A few initial flakes quickly increased until we found ourselves struggling in a merciless blizzard that all but obliterated the highway. What we had never done before on these homeward excursions was to spend a night in a motel. Fortunately, a mile or two down the road we approached a village with a gas station, an ancient hotel, and an Elks Lodge.

When we asked for a room at the local hotel, a prim, elderly lady, the proprietor, whom we learned was a very devout Catholic, informed us that due to the sudden change in weather she had only one remaining room. Since we were a mixed party, it would not do for us to sleep together in a single room. Such an arrangement was absolutely out of the question. I decided now it would be appropriate to show our true colors. "Madam," I began, looking as pious as possible, "we understand the problem. We are, believe it or not, ministerial students. The girls in our group are missionary children from Colombia, South America. We have been driving two days, non-stop, without rest. Believe me; you can trust us to behave ourselves."

Up to this point, she had been eyeing us with obvious suspicion but now her features softened. "We have an idea," I went on. "We'll hang a blanket up across the middle of the room. Boys on one side, girls on the other, and we promise we will be good." Now I saw the hint of a smile on her lips. She finally relented.

"I don't usually allow this, but there is just no other room. Passengers arriving are now being housed in the Elks Lodge. I guess I'll let you have the room." Bless her!

When we woke up the next morning, the sun was shining. The highway had been plowed. Refreshed after a good night's sleep and a great breakfast, we piled back into the sleek blue Cadillac and headed for home singing, "Oh, what a beautiful morning."

By the 1950s, another generation of Ernys began appearing in the hallowed halls of Asbury College. First came my brother, Bob, from California, after attending Pasadena College for two years. I arrived two years later, entering the class of '57, the Torchbearers.

Following me came my Uncle Ed Erny's daughter, Carol, from National City, California, where her father was a pastor at a large Methodist church.

Coming to Asbury from my home in California put me in an entirely different world, one that from the start was surprisingly congenial and comfortable. The campus gave me the feeling that this is where I belonged, where I was destined to be.

I had thought that my many years as a child in boarding school in the Himalayas, far removed from my parents, would inure me to any future homesickness. This was not entirely the case. Asbury was a friendly enough campus, but I did not know a soul, and my home at 831 North Hobart in Los Angeles was over half a continent away.

My one solace was that Uncle Meredith Helsby, Mother's brother, and Aunt Christine lived just off campus in a house that served as sort of an OMS regional center. The Helsbys had earlier been missionaries in both China and India, and for a term were our neighbors on the Allahabad seminary campus.

So when I knocked at the door of the white framed house at 401 Kenyon Avenue, I received the kind of welcome reserved for favorite kin. Meredith was away from home most of the time in mission deputation. Aunt Christine, a true southern belle, had the gift of hospitality, and her lively brood, Sandra, Gary, and Sheryl, treated me like a big brother. Christine appreciated adult company and the help I provided in shoveling coal for the furnace in the winter.

The house was happily furnished with a TV, much appreciated in this era when television was not allowed on campus or in any of the dorm rooms. We enjoyed watching Nelson Eddy and Jeanette MacDonald in some of their old classic productions: *Indian Love Call, Rose-Marie,* and *Give Me Some Men Who Are Stouthearted Men.*

In the post-war boom, colleges and universities had record student enrollments with many attending college on the GI bill. Additional dorms were required, and quickly. Old Quonset huts on the edge of the campus became makeshift residences, and nearby was the recently constructed Johnson Hall, named for the college president, Z.T. Johnson. The three-story edifice looked impressive enough, but hasty construction combined with limited available funds resulted in a building with considerable shortcomings. For instance, when showers were in great demand, especially early in the morning and just prior to special occasions like the Artist Series (concerts featuring well-known artists), a problem developed. There was a reasonable flow of water on the lower floors but hardly a trickle reached the third floor where I had been assigned to number 315, a corner room.

This room was somewhat larger than others and for that reason housed not the usual two students but three. Fortunately, in those days we traveled light. I arrived, as did my roommates, with a large suitcase or footlocker, containing most of my earthly goods.

My roommates in Johnson Hall had already settled in by the time I arrived that fall. The first to introduce himself was Earl Andrews, a southerner from Dothan, Alabama, destined to be a lifelong friend. Earl proved to be the friendliest, most amenable soul one could ever meet. He was a freshman, and I was a transfer sophomore. He had enrolled earlier for the summer quarter at which time he worked on the college farm to pay for his tuition.

My other roommate was a senior and local Kentuckian, Grant Nealis. A senior rooming with two newcomers was practically unheard of. Later Grant told us that after his first three years and several roommates, "I felt somehow that God wanted me to make a change and to specify no particular persons. I would just leave that to the college and Divine Providence." Thus, he gained two roommates totally unknown to him and developed friendships which would dramatically affect his life.

Grant was as friendly and outgoing as I was shy. He had considerable leadership gifts and had been student body president his senior year in Lexington's outstanding Henry Clay High School. Being an older and experienced senior, I looked to him to acquaint me with campus personnel and rules. I was shocked when one night I accompanied him to the college grill for a snack. Passing one of the campus beauties, he remarked in a voice loud enough for everyone to hear, "Hi, Barb. My dream is to wake up Christmas morning and find you in my stocking."

Grant's eye for beauty became apparent the moment one entered our dorm room. He was an excellent photographer and landed a job on the yearbook staff. In the process of shooting a great many photos for the annual, he also managed closeups of Asbury's most beautiful coeds, particularly one uncommonly gorgeous young lady. Soon our room became a regular stopping place for many of our dorm neighbors.

There's a sense in which the campuses of all evangelical

Christian colleges are very much alike with congenial friendships and the camaraderie of a body of believers. Though I still retain a genuine appreciation for Pasadena College, from my first semester in 1954 at Asbury, I sensed a depth of spirituality on the campus such as I had seldom encountered elsewhere. I ascribe this partly to the 1950 revival, the influence of which was still lingering over the school, like a mist tarrying over a bluegrass meadow in the early morning.

At Asbury, there were the requisite prayers before every class and major events. Class prayer meetings were held Wednesday evenings. More than this, some of my fellow schoolmates had a passion for prayer. When two Evangelical Methodist students in my dorm discovered that I had attended the first established Evangelical Methodist Church in Los Angeles, they invited me to meet with them every week for prayer. Together we read E.M. Bounds' *Preacher in Prayer* and then knelt to earnestly voice our petitions.

CHAPTER 6

MY FIRST PREACHING

For many of us, weekends at Asbury extended from Saturday noon through Monday. Classes resumed on Tuesday morning. This schedule was designed to enable students to take major roles in a variety of Christian activities, from visitation at hospitals, jails, and other state institutions to the pastoring of small local churches, often called chapels, of which there were quite a number within an hour's drive of the campus.

In addition, there was the very visible presence of the "Sallies," members of the Salvation Army on the campus. I had, of course, heard of the heroics of the early Salvation Army heroes, General William and Catherine Booth and their dynamic, gifted daughter, Evangeline. But the only Salvation Army activities I had witnessed in the Los Angeles area involved the collection of used clothing for sale in the downtown store. I had never realized Asbury was the organization's officially approved college for the schooling of their youth. It was not long before I encountered an entirely different kind of Salvation Army personnel than I had ever known existed. The appointed campus recruiter for their weekend activities at their post in Frankfort, the capital of Kentucky, was a young man of Chinese extraction, Wing Ching.

Wing was an annoyingly exuberant brother, forever recruiting volunteers for the Salvation Army street meetings. I learned that after the meetings they would accost derelicts in the slums and witness to them. I could only imagine the zealous goings-on during these weekend excursions. I politely declined his invitations to join the team and learned to prepare credible excuses beforehand. By winter term, I was running out of excuses, and Wing's persistent invitations continued unabated. It was clear that I would never be rid of this gentleman until I had agreed, at least once, to participate in the street meetings in Frankfort.

So it was one Saturday afternoon in February that I found myself wedged into a small Chevy bound for the state capital, Frankfort, Kentucky. The Salvation Army Corps Center was situated behind the courthouse, about three blocks from the tenderloin district, which was at that time fittingly dubbed "the bottoms." In these pre-mall times, country folk flooded into town on Saturday afternoons to shop and seek entertainment. Scores of them did little more than gather on the big lawn in front of the courthouse to chat with friends and acquaintances.

The Army had arranged with authorities to occupy the street corner directly across from the courthouse. While the officers set up loudspeakers, others in uniform made visits to nearby establishments, particularly taverns and bars where, curiously, they were always welcomed to sell copies of their magazine, *The War Cry.*

As soon as it was time for the street meeting to commence, Bill Dearen took charge. His parents were Army officers in New York, and he himself was dressed in a smart red and black uniform and hat. Bill began the service with cheery words of welcome and a bold call to listen to the gospel. One by one, our team members formed a line beside Bill on the curb. Altogether, there were seven or eight of us students.

Salvationists often grow up learning to play a brass instrument and together they constitute some of the finest brass bands in the world. At Asbury, we had the lusty trombone of

MY FIRST PREACHING

Paul Rader and the dulcet cornet of Tom Gabrielsen. Mention must also be made of the drummer whose huge instrument was usually laid on the sidewalk after services and used as an altar.

As the lively music pealed out with "Ring the Bells of Heaven," a small crowd gathered around. A short sermon was followed by testimony time from which no one was exempt. Fortunately, I was situated at the end of the line. After six students, I calculated, the ice would be broken before it became my turn.

Though I was a missionary kid, few of our team knew it. I had never before witnessed publicly on a street corner. I realized now that a desperate emergency prayer was very much in order. It went something like this: *Lord, how did I ever get in this mess? You'll have to tell me what to say. If I get through this, I'll never again keep company with these crazy Sallies.* The name "Sally" especially described the girls with their old-fashioned black bonnets, harking back to the time of Evangeline Booth, the founder of the Salvation Army in the United States.

I cannot remember a single thing I said in my first outdoor testimony on the corner that day. I do recall the marvelous sense of relief when I was done and the service came to a close. My relief was short-lived, however, for immediately after the closing prayer I found myself looking into the smiling face of Bill, our leader.

"Ed," he began, "we're going to the bottoms tonight after supper and we want you to preach for that service." I was stunned and terrified. I could feel my knees tremble under my gray overcoat (the first one I ever owned, having grown up in India and southern California). No appropriate excuse came to mind. I swallowed. Finally, I heard myself saying, "Well, I guess so. Okay, I'll try." I didn't tell Bill I had never before preached on a street corner or anywhere else for that matter.

The local corps, headed by Commissioner Richardson, was unique in that it provided overnight accommodations for up to a dozen or so weekend student workers. Mrs. Richardson, assisted by a few of the girls, always prepared a hearty supper, often spaghetti.

Some of the regular weekend volunteers were secretly dating one another, and weekends at Frankfort furnished a convenient venue for spending time together. It was here that my brother, Bob, and Phyllis McLaughlin, from Mansfield, Ohio, really got their romance going.

At seven o'clock that evening, I found myself flanked by my new Salvation Army buddies standing in front of the Blue Moon Tavern in the heart of the bottoms, a poorer section of the city. A small crowd gathered, mostly curious observers who had nowhere in particular to go.

Behind me, looking out the second-floor windows of the ramshackle Blue Moon Tavern, were young girls, bedraggled and giggling, with painted faces and scarlet fingernails, sure marks of their profession. Shortly, a disheveled man shuffled by and, looking up and spotting a female acquaintance, he leered, "Hey, Suzie, why don't you come up to my room tonight?"

She disdainfully refused with "Are you kidding, Frank? I know what you want."

And over her protest Frank went on. "Now, Suzie, I ain't putting you on. We'll have a good time. You know, talk. I just bought a six-pack and that's the truth."

By this time, the trombone was playing a favorite Army tune, which was our signal to begin. Since Bill's sudden invitation that afternoon, I had been wracking my brain over what to say. This would be my first real sermon. Then I remembered Dad's favorite text, also one I had memorized at Culter Academy, Romans 1:16: *For I am not ashamed of the gospel of Christ: for it is the power of God unto salvation.*

Following the usual singing and three testimonies, I stepped up to the microphone. I surveyed my listeners and found myself addressing a most depressing collection of human beings, habitués of the streets and, of course, some patrons of the Blue Moon Tavern. So there we were in the very place that respectable people tell their children to never go near.

Was there any hope for these human wrecks? We later learned that among this vagrant flotsam that evening was a one-time medical student at the University of Kentucky, until drinking turned him into a besotted bum. Then it came to me with sudden force. Why was I not ashamed of the gospel? Because I realized that for the likes of these ruined souls, these drifters, castoffs on the evil tides of human society, any other message is a useless joke. There is no telling them, "Do better; think of your family; give up the bottle; try to be respectable; work hard and get an education; find a decent job." All such admonitions had proven futile. Only one hope remains, and that is the cross, a glorious hope of which I was not ashamed.

Soon enough the service was over. I had survived. Some even congratulated me on a wonderful sermon. A few bums lingered for a word of sympathy, a prayer, perhaps a handout. Time to head back to the Army Corps, where we would be spending the night.

Our labors, however, I soon discovered were far from finished. My friend Bill appeared again, this time with a bundle of gospel tracts. "What do we do now?" I asked timidly. He cut the stack of tracts in two and gave me half.

"Now," he smiled, "we hit the taverns." What he meant by "hit the taverns" I could only imagine. Then, seriously, he said, "Ed, I should tell you that this is not a safe district at night, but I'm wearing the uniform. You stay close to me and you will be all right." I was only too happy to oblige.

Growing up in India, the poorest nation in Asia, I had seen some pretty seedy dives along the back alleys of Allahabad and Calcutta. But what confronted me now were scenes of the sort I had only read about. On Saturday nights, the dregs of Frankfort made their unsteady way to this part of town. Ear-splitting, raucous country music in this pre-rock-and-roll era poured out of the houses of ill repute, advertising that the evening entertainment was in full swing. Patrons, well lubricated, crowded the dance floor. Others sat in narrow booths huddled over a drink and laughing with a forced hilarity calculated to convince themselves that they were "having a good time."

I kept close to Bill as he pushed his way through the crowd, putting gospel booklets in the hands of distracted patrons. These offerings were seldom rejected, which surprised me. This was some years before the Four Spiritual Laws and Evangelism Explosion techniques had become popular. Bill's opening line was, "I'd like to give you this gospel tract." This usually elicited a low grunt and, occasionally, less than a sincere thanks. Bill followed up with a blunt "Are you a Christian, sir?" The slightest hesitation was Bill's opening for a brief explanation of the plan of salvation and then, "Have you ever received Christ as your Savior?"

Staying close to Bill, watching, listening, I soon got the hang of it. Slipping a booklet from the stack, while inwardly uttering a prayer for boldness, I began launching into "Sir, I would like to give you this gospel tract," all the time maneuvering so as to keep Bill within earshot. By the time we "hit" our third tavern, I was convinced that in that swirling tangle of derelicts there was likely not a soul who wanted to hear any preaching about being saved. Often we heard "I'm a Baptist. I got saved and baptized when I was a kid" or some such statement.

Leaning against a bar, three doors down from the Blue Moon, I met Jerry. He was starting on his first drink and was still clear-eyed and articulate. I judged him to be in his early twenties. He told me that he worked in a local brewery. He listened with surprising interest to my gospel presentation, and I

MY FIRST PREACHING

saw that his eyes were now misty. "Jerry," I said, "have you ever received Christ as your Savior?" He shook his head. "Wouldn't you like to do that tonight?" I went on, "right now?"

"Yes," he nodded. "I'd like you to pray for me." Bill suggested we walk the two blocks to the Salvation Army Chapel where the atmosphere would be considerably more conducive to prayer.

The small chapel was located in the basement of the Corps. In it was a collection of worn-out chairs, a pulpit, and an altar padded with cheap brown plastic. As we proceeded to the front, Jerry hurried forward and suddenly threw himself onto the altar rail. Bill and I prayed for Jerry and then asked if he would like to pray as well. He nodded his head and started in.

I knew in an instant that somewhere in Jerry's past there had been a church, probably Sunday school, and very likely a praying mother. Prayer gushed out of his mouth like an erupting geyser. He confessed his sin, calling with vehemence on the Savior to have mercy on his poor, lost soul. I opened my eyes to see Jerry's tears flowing freely down the altar, creating a large puddle on the padded leatherette, which in time overflowed and ran down both sides of that altar rail.

With the completion of that prayer came a sudden hallelujah, a mark of absolute assurance that another lost sinner had come back to the Father's house. We all stood and embraced. Jerry's visage was transformed as though someone had planted a thousand-watt bulb right in his skull.

The next week I received a letter from Jerry. He told me that he had truly been saved and had started back to church.

That night the Asbury team bunked in the Salvation Army dorm that Richardson had built in the basement. I was assigned a top bunk and was soon being entertained by the assorted noises of young men all in the throes of deep slumber. Tired as I was, for some reason, most of the night I lay as wide-awake as I could ever remember being. There came a dawning consciousness that leading a lost soul to Christ was probably the most gratifying thing I had ever done in my entire life, far more exciting than scoring a touchdown that Friday afternoon in Flintridge. Before morning I was convinced that there could be absolutely nothing more exciting, gratifying, or invigorating than devoting my entire life to telling the world about Jesus. I felt like Scrooge in *A Christmas Carol* who, upon waking from the final encounter with the ghosts of Christmas, ecstatically cried, "I'm so happy! I'm as giddy as a schoolboy! I have no right to be this happy!"

The rest of that weekend I was possessed by an exquisite joy, the joy of a totally new discovery. That Sunday, more street meetings were scheduled along with a gospel service in the local workhouse. I was no longer nervous. Instead, I felt as though I was in my element, doing what I was created to do.

CHAPTER 7

CAMPUS ACTIVITIES

During my sophomore year, several classmates returned from Japan, where they had spent over two years in an OMS evangelism program, Every Creature Crusade (now called Every Community for Christ), to continue their college studies. Among them was Lowell Williamson, the son of Everett Williamson, one of Cowman's original band of young men who joined OMS in 1917 to help complete the first crusade in Japan called the Great Village Campaign.

Lowell and other crusaders, fresh from the field, were endued with a contagious enthusiasm for evangelizing Asia. They now became the amazingly effective recruiters of the next generation of crusaders. Lowell had pastored for several years in Ohio before enlisting in the second crusade. An effective and experienced preacher, he kept busy almost every weekend speaking in churches in Kentucky, Ohio, and Illinois. For these weekend mission excursions, he sought traveling companions to help with the driving and provide companionship. All weekend, he would expose the young men who traveled with him to the challenge of joining the crusade. I traveled with Lowell on occasion, little dreaming that in the future, he and his future wife, Naomi Bletcher, a classmate, would be our neighbors for almost twenty years in Taiwan with Lowell as our field director for much of that time.

I introduced Grant, my roommate, to Lowell and other OMSers on campus. Lowell invited Grant to travel with him for weekend meetings. When Dale McClain, one of OMS' most dynamic speakers, came to Asbury that spring, he challenged young men to join in the crusade adventure. After the service, half a dozen or more Asburians made appointments to talk with him.

By the following spring of 1955, Lowell's efforts had borne fruit. Grant applied to join the Every Creature Crusade and began his two-and-a-half-year term that fall. We talked for hours about OMS, still a new organization to him, and prayed earnestly for his needed funds. I helped him design a prayer card to assist in funding.

The spiritual tone on campus in those days was high, fostering a great variety of Christian activities. With my background, I was also much involved in Student Volunteers, the remnant of the nationwide missionary movement. At Asbury, however, the missions impulse was still thriving. The room where we met was full each Thursday at noon and resounded with the strains of the song "Send the Light" and moving testimonies of God's call. Here student leaders focused on missionary enterprises around the world.

Probably one-quarter of all the students during our era had announced their intention to enter Christian ministry, as pastors, evangelists, church workers, or missionaries. For the Ministerial Association meetings held each month, Talbot Chapel was filled.

During my student days, no intercollegiate sports existed at Asbury, although intramural sports were permitted. At Pasadena College, where I had spent my freshman year, the campus culture was nearly dominated by athletics, and the most favored and influential campus leaders were usually athletes. For me, this marked an important difference between the two schools.

At Asbury, it did not take me long to get over my early homesickness. Painfully shy, I did not make acquaintances as readily as most. I tried out for the class intramural basketball team, but the practices took too much time and my chances of making the talented Torchbearer squad were slim. Even if I made the team, I reasoned, I would not be playing much. Thus ended my basketball career, a shock to oldsters who still remembered Dad's unparalleled career at Asbury. Dad's classmates and other alumni told me, "Your father, for a little man, was the best basketball player I ever saw."

I had earlier learned to play tennis and loved the game dearly. In time, it verged on a passion, one that required some restraint. I had never had the benefit of tennis lessons or coaching and had developed bad form, which I spent much of my life attempting to correct. The old Asbury courts, made of rough cement, tore up the balls in a set or two, and replacing them was an expense I could not afford. Still, we had great fun – whether with my roommate Earl, or Tom Gabrielsen, who had been a high school champion in the Chicago area.

The tennis season at the college during these years consisted of a single tournament in the spring. Tom was the college champ my senior year, but I bested him the following year, my first year of seminary. Tom was a deceptively good player, not flashy, but a kind of human backboard.

I should mention that the one frustration for me with this sport was an incredible rule that in this modern era would be quite beyond reason. The college handbook stated that all players were required to wear long pants. Strangely, at the same time the men were on the tennis court in long pants, in the adjacent gym, the girls' basketball teams were enjoying the freedom of shorts. When I pointed out this inconsistency to college authorities, I was informed that in 1927, Bill Tilden always wore long pants while playing at Wimbledon, so no further inquiries into this subject would be welcomed.

There were other campus regulations during this period which elicited frequent complaints. Freshmen and sophomores, apart from ministerial students, could not have automobiles. This, of course, seriously curtailed one's social life.

For underclassmen, on a limited number of occasions, on-campus dates were permitted – to prayer meetings, concerts, school plays, and especially the annual Artist Series. At Asbury, girls almost always outnumbered boys. For major social events, many of the girls attended unaccompanied, while others stayed in their rooms, praying for a date at some future event.

The attention of the faculty was drawn to this sad situation, and our much-esteemed and beloved dean of men, Y.D. Westerfield, called a meeting of all the young men. He good-naturedly encouraged us to pay more attention to the fairer sex and, above all, to provide them dates for major social occasions.

During that first year, there was no female acquaintance of mine whom I felt comfortable taking to the principal events of the college year. By my junior year, however, I knew a few classmates well enough to engage their company for the Artist Series. In my senior year, I enjoyed a happy and permanent solution.

Most chronicles of campus life are replete with antidotes of misdemeanors. Alas, my disposition has always been law abiding and thus makes my chronicle dull reading. One incident, however, does remain in my recollection of those beloved college days.

Some of the regulations back then, from this present perspective, seem almost incredible. Most unpopular was the 10:00 p.m. curfew. Promptly at this hour, without exception, every student was to be in his dorm room in bed with the lights out. Two gentlemen, usually older married students, were employed as night watchmen, presumably to secure the campus buildings and watch for any nocturnal student mischief. In the early evening, the primary miscreants were couples wandering the campus holding hands or sitting in various obscure corners.

Later in the evening, the watchmen were alert to curfew violations. A light on in any dorm window spelled a demerit for all students inhabiting that room. Rule breakers with lights on or caught sneaking off campus were in for an appointment with the school DC (Discipline Committee).

One evening that first semester, Grant proposed that we drive into Lexington for ice cream. I naively replied, "We can't go off campus this late. We have to be in bed by ten o'clock."

"No problem," he smiled. "Just follow me." Then he grabbed his portable radio, turned it up to a high volume, and headed out the front door of Johnson Dorm with me in tow. Passing the night watchmen to the accompaniment of loud music, he offered a casual greeting and headed for the parking lot and his 1950 Nash.

"We really shouldn't be doing this," I ventured.

"It's okay," he said. "These guys are my friends." Grant drove halfway to Lexington to a well-known establishment where we enjoyed a repast of banana splits.

Back in the dorm that night, my conscience offended, I asked Grant again about the rule pertaining to staying up after 10:00 p.m. and going off campus. His jovial reply was "The way I figure it, what are rules for if not to be broken!"

CHAPTER 8

SHELBYVILLE

In the spring of 1955, near the end of my first year at Asbury, my roommate Earl confronted me with a proposition. He had been assisting a classmate, Hal Edwards, in pastoring a small chapel in Shelbyville, Kentucky, a city located about twenty miles southeast of Louisville. Hal, the senior pastor, had resigned, leaving Earl with the full responsibility for the chapel, and he asked if I would help him in pastoring the church. By this time, I had gained some preaching and personal evangelism experience on the streets of Frankfurt with the Salvation Army. Thanks to this experience I could tell Earl, yes, I would be his associate pastor at Peoples Chapel. "Well then," he said, "we'll be co-pastors." *Wait a minute*, I thought. *Co-pastors? Me? A pastor of a church at eighteen?* That was incredible. I had never dreamed of such a thing.

The small Shelbyville chapel had been born in the wake of the Asbury revival of 1950 and founded by Jack Paschal, an older man with a prison record. He had rented the local theater Sunday mornings and came very near to filling it each week. His parishioners had been mostly people of questionable backgrounds and lower incomes. Jack had written his life story in a book he titled *From Prison Bars to Shining Stars*, which had circulated throughout that area.

After some months, the chapel attendance fell off, and Jack

moved his congregation down the street to a hall situated directly above the Odd Fellows Lodge. In time, he prevailed upon the Asbury Ministerial Association to take over the Shelbyville Peoples Chapel. It bothered me that the name he had chosen, "Peoples," in those years had strong overtones of Marx, Lenin, and the Communist Party, a fact that was likely unknown to most of the chapel members.

My brother, Bob, who at the time was attending seminary across the street from the college, joined the pastoral team as well.

Pastoring the Shelbyville church involved far more than holding a solitary Sunday service and then heading back to the campus. The pattern had been set by Fletcher Hardy, a previous pastor of the chapel and still a legend whose exploits were recounted to us with annoying regularity.

We would arrive at Shelbyville on Saturday afternoon in time to hold an open-air meeting on Main Street in front of the Rexall Drug Store, which graciously provided a hookup for the PA system. Saturday evening was billed as the main evangelistic service of the weekend. Prior to Sunday school the next morning came the weekly jail service. The old town clink was located just down the road from the chapel. We were expected there each week. The great iron cage opened for us to face the company of the weekly drunks availing themselves of the hospitality of the jail for an overnight in the lone, very crowded cell.

Following the jail service, we walked the three blocks back to the chapel where superintendent Lister King had started the preliminaries for the morning Sunday school. Bob and I took turns teaching the older youth. Immediately after this came the worship service and then Sunday dinner. Unfortunately, this sumptuous meal had usually been prepared much earlier and by now was quite cold. After dinner, we made our way to the edge of town to the prominent Old Masons Home where the residents welcomed us warmly. Then we visited local shut-ins before returning to the chapel for the final Sunday evening service.

Finally, we began the long drive home, a trip that averaged about an hour and a half. Though tired, we and the classmates who had volunteered their musical talents were usually in an exuberant mood. In my old, utterly unreliable '41 Dodge, we would burst into song. Our favorite and most appropriate chorus was "I Feel Like Traveling On," followed by "Heaven Came Down and Glory Filled My Soul."

Since the weekend services at Shelbyville required our presence from Saturday afternoon until Sunday evening, we had to find overnight lodging on Saturdays. One of the members was actually assigned the task of arranging accommodations for us but was often remiss in doing this. Hence, upon arrival in town, it was up to us pastors to get on the phone and call various members, prevailing upon them to furnish beds for the night. Most were cordial and invited us with a warm welcome. Others, by long pauses and hesitation in their reply, signaled that they viewed our request as most inconvenient and even an imposition.

We often found lodging with the Bentleys or the Kings. George Bentley was a most cordial gentleman, his wife a good cook, and his two daughters made regular musical contributions to the chapel. They lived on a small farm at the edge of town. Their old farmhouse was bereft of central heating. The cooking was done on a wood-burning stove, and in the adjacent living room was the pot-bellied stove. Close by in another room was the large feather bed and, with the door opened, some warmth was channeled to us through winter nights.

The Bentley girls, Betty and Martha Ray, were both in high school. Martha was the chapel pianist, and Betty helped with Sunday school and occasionally song leading.

Our other provider of bed and breakfast was the Sunday school superintendent, Lister King, a local builder and the only man of means in the congregation. Subdivisions were sprouting in the outskirts of Shelbyville, and King had gained a reputation as a man who could put up a fine three-bedroom home with hardwood floors in six days.

When we arrived to pastor the chapel, the Kings had just moved into a new home. We knew that when we stayed with the Kings one of us would have to share a bed with Uncle Billy. He was, we learned, Lister's cousin, a man who was virtually speechless and had a mysterious past. Our second year in Shelbyville, a parishioner divulged a King family secret. Uncle Billy was a murderer. For reasons still unclear, he had killed his wife and served a term in the penitentiary. Due to his mild and gentle nature and perhaps some extenuating circumstances, he was remanded to Lister's custody, where he lived the remainder of his life with gratitude and grace.

During my two years at Shelbyville, we saw a good number of people come forward to the altar to find forgiveness and salvation. For one of these people, Jimmie, who was mentally disabled, this was a regular occurrence every Sunday night. Perhaps the most memorable of our converts was Clara Lambert, an orphaned teenager from Indiana, now living with her sister and truck-driver husband. One night with our friend Helmut Schultz preaching, Clara came weeping to the altar to receive Christ. The transformation was immediate and glorious.

We arranged to have Clara enrolled in Kentucky Mountain Christian High School, located in bloody Breathitt County, so named because of its lawlessness. Arriving on campus, we were met by the administrator, a large matronly woman with a no-nonsense air. We explained that Clara came from Shelbyville. With a wry smile and in a sotto voce, the woman said, "Can any good thing come out of Shelbyville?" Then, as if to confirm her discouraging prognosis, after a very few weeks our prize convert, Clara, for some reason we never learned of, was shipped home to Shelbyville.

Clara returned to church and seemed repentant, but a year later disappeared with a local boy of doubtful reputation. Their fling ended suddenly for Clara. A week later, tearfully, she informed us that she had been deserted by her new boyfriend who had so shamefully used her.

This story, so typical of young girls from poor families, has a wonderfully happy ending. In Taiwan, we received the news that dear Clara had gotten right with the Lord, married Elwood, an older man who ran a carpet store. They joined a local church and became stalwarts, much appreciated by the congregation. They also raised a fine daughter. She and her husband have blessed them with grandchildren who now, with Elwood deceased, bring great joy to Clara.

The Shouses lived in a cubbyhole between the health office and an old apartment building. Their home consisted of a single room with an adjoining kitchen and bathroom. A sprawling double bed occupied almost the entire area, allowing only space for an easy chair and a small table for dining.

These dear people had married young and had numerous offspring. By the time they were in their late teens, their family began growing by one addition a year. When we arrived, the Shouses were a sizable clan. All these children seemed to marry young and felt it their immediate duty to replenish the earth. Everywhere we went in Shelbyville we ran into members of the prolific family. Mom and Pa Shouse were not only great-great-grandparents but always, it seemed, were about to add yet another generation to their patrimony.

Amazingly, all who knew Mama Shouse agreed that she was the sweetest, most patient, and most spiritual soul they had ever known. Her eyes twinkled with delight. She loved the

Bible and the old hymns and cooked about the best southern fried chicken we had ever eaten. It seems that her angelic nature and saintly traits were the result of fifty-five years of marriage to the most cantankerous man in Shelbyville.

Pa Shouse had never, in living memory, been free of complaints about his physical health. We learned that one sure way to ruin his day was to comment on how well he looked. His delight was to field our questions about his immediate health. In reply, he began reciting an interminable list of afflictions, disorders, and sundry complaints. "Naw," he would end with. "I ain't doing well at all, not a bit. I just been to the doctor again." His litany of complaints usually ended with a long face and a longer than necessary description of his hernia, hemorrhoids, and varicose veins.

Then, although too sick to go to church, he had accumulated a long list of convictions and offenses against the church. There was the evil of "painted" women and Jezebels in the church who wore slacks. Missionary slide shows were another offense that turned church into a worldly movie theater. "When I go to the doctor's," he informed us, "they have a telly-vision in the waiting room. I won't enter that room facing forwards. I back into that-there lounge so I can't even see the Devil's box."

Former pastors and I have a treasury of antidotes of discoveries and happenings in Shelbyville. Many of these involve our dismal lack of money. I had bought my old Dodge from a car dealer, Wayne McKinley, for a price I could afford. The best that he could do for me was a vehicle with four bald tires. The clutch was already slipping. The heater, which promised warmth with the appearance of a red light under the dash, was in fact not functioning at all. Trouble, without exaggeration, was a weekly occurrence. I resorted to a junkyard where I could pick up practically treadless replacement tires for two dollars apiece. I developed great skill at changing flats, an art that was to serve me well in the future during the Taiwan crusade.

Almost every weekend we invited college friends to join us in Shelbyville. They would help with song leading, piano playing, and preaching. One of the first was Helmut Schultz. He had recently returned from Japan where he had served with the Every Creature Crusade. One weekend we insisted that Helmut join us for the meetings in Shelbyville. He asked if he could also bring along Norma Jean Hickerson, a young lady he was courting at the time, in a relationship that showed considerable promise. Of course, we agreed. When we left the campus that Saturday, I was aware that the clutch on my Dodge was slipping badly. Still, with patience and prayer, we made it over the sixty miles of Kentucky hills to our destination.

The Sunday evening service did not end until 10:00 p.m. due to an encouraging altar service after Helmut's message. Happily, Helmut, Norma Jean, Bob, and I then piled into my car. Aware of the increasingly unreliable condition of the clutch, I asked for prayer, and we began the trip back to campus. Soon, however, the clutch began giving signs of total demise, particularly on steep inclines.

We resorted to a procedure I had heard of for occasions such as this. Norma Jean would steer, and the three of us young men would jump out, get behind the car, and push. Once the car topped the hill and began to gather speed, we would jump back into the vehicle. The added weight helped sustain momentum, enabling the car to make it almost halfway up the next hill, whereupon at my signal we would again jump out and push with all our might.

This was a tricky business at 11:00 p.m. on a dark highway with traffic whizzing by. Utilizing these desperate measures of locomotion, an hour later we finally pulled into Lawrenceville, about halfway home. All of us agreed the car would not likely make it back to campus.

The only business still open past midnight was a small local hotel. We parked the hapless Dodge by the curb, and I telephoned a friend, imploring him to come and rescue us. As we gloomily waited in that small hotel lobby, I offered Helmut profuse apologies for this embarrassing turn of events. To my surprise, he immediately draped his big arm over my shoulder and escorted me to an adjacent hallway.

He then faced me with a big smile. "Don't apologize, Ed," he said. "This is the very thing I've been praying for. I'm thinking of marrying Norma Jean," he whispered. "I've been asking God for some really difficult experience to test her. It's important that I see if she is missionary material. Tonight God has answered that prayer." The next week I learned that Helmut and Norma Jean were engaged.

Soon our help arrived and ferried us all back to our dorms. The following day I returned to Lawrenceville and had my old Dodge interred in a local junkyard.

CHAPTER 9

A NEW CHALLENGE

There occurred another surprising and most improbable event near the end of my sophomore year. Don Grant, a much-admired man on campus and one of my classmates, knew that our dads had been together in the class of 1925. Don's father had often mentioned my dad's leadership gifts.

Given this information, and though he barely knew me, Don concluded that I would be a good choice for president of our Torchbearer class the following year. Without consulting me, he made a speech containing some incredible claims and half-truths, insisting that this newcomer should be class leader. I was shocked and appalled, but due to his eloquence, I found myself as the president of the Torchbearer class of 1955-56.

At Yosemite that summer, I mulled over the fix that I was in. There would be class business meetings and prayer meetings that I would be responsible for, to say nothing of the imposing junior class play and the Junior-Senior Banquet. I sincerely regretted the circumstances that had brought me to this dilemma, and during the summer, I pored over *Robert's Rules of Order*. In my new role as president of the Torchbearer class, I worked with a great many classmates and, in the process, made new acquaintances, some of whom became dear friends.

I look back on that junior year as perhaps the busiest of my entire life. In addition to my presidential class responsibilities,

I wrote a weekly column for *The Collegian*, the official student newspaper. It also was my responsibility to promote and fund an ambitious class project, which called for a professional recording of Asbury College chapel music. This recording was to be sold to students and alumni and would hopefully garner money for the junior class projects.

I was also on the staff of the college yearbook and did much of the writing. In those days, the yearbook was entirely the responsibility of the junior class. I recall again and again returning to the campus after a weekend of ministry, my head spinning, and asking myself, "What do I do next?" I soon learned to make a daily "to do" list to which I constantly referred, organizing the day's chores in the order of priority. This served me well in future years on the mission field when I faced many demands on my time.

Assignments also came from my speech and drama professors, Jim Young, Art Fleser, and Gladys Greathouse. Jim urged me to enter the statewide oratorical speech contest to be held at Berea College that spring. Naomi Bletcher, who took second place, and I represented the college.

The subject of my oration was "Total Abstinence," a speech I had already given to the local WCTU (Woman's Christian Temperance Union). A student who was a natural orator was the undisputed champion on the men's side. I came in an unspectacular third, perhaps impeded by the subject, which did not find much favor in America's most notable whiskey and bourbon state.

Later in the year, Jim Young persuaded me to enter a statewide playwriting contest. My play, *Without the Gate*, inspired by my childhood in India, took second place. We went to the University of Kentucky in Lexington to see the drama performed in the student theater. Jim later staged the drama at

Taylor University where he was teaching. I was told that it was well received.

Before I leave the subject of drama, I must mention *Plus Power*, a film produced entirely by Asbury College students that following year. My gifted classmate, Joe Hale, had just returned from a mission in Thailand. He borrowed an excellent German movie camera from a fellow student. Then he asked me and a number of other students to take a screen test. To my amazement, I was chosen for the lead in this short movie, featuring a young man who chooses God's call to the ministry over the affections of a beautiful girl. This was my first and last experience in movie acting.

During the final semester of my junior year, I was amazed to learn that several of my classmates were intent on entering my name on the ballot for student body president for the following year. I was genuinely surprised, because I had never viewed my efforts as junior class president as anything worthy of much notice. Bob Bradford would run with me as the vice president. Our junior year he was editor of the yearbook, and I had the privilege of working closely with him. Bob was an older pre-med student and a Korean War veteran.

When the votes were counted, I was truly amazed to hear my name announced as the winner. Bewildered, I thought to myself, *Do these kids, most of whom hardly know me, have any idea what they have done?* My running mate, Bob, did not garner enough votes for the vice-presidency. Instead, I was paired with Henry Grayson, a very handsome and gifted classmate, whom I knew well since he was also the vice president of the junior class.

With summer came another pilgrimage to Yosemite to resume my job in the huge Camp Curry dining room. My thoughts were now focused on the coming school year with the many terrifying responsibilities that would fall to me.

The faculty of Asbury College consisted for the most part of sacrificially dedicated men and women with a genuine and enduring love for their students. I developed rich friendships with a number of them. One such professor was Dr. Cecil Hamann. He was a respected scientist and was a valuable and sympathetic friend to all pre-med students striving mightily for their placement in a medical college upon graduation. Science was never my forte, and I always felt I never fulfilled the expectations of this dear man who knew and honored my father.

Without a doubt, my favorite professor was Dr. Frances White. Upon my arrival, I had declared an English major. This was my favorite subject in high school where dear Mrs. Thompson had taken notice of my poetry and encouraged me to pursue creative writing. She also guided me through the thicket of English grammar, a course I had never taken due to a gap between my Woodstock school year and the first term of high school in the U.S.

Frances opened up to me the rich vein of classical English literature, all the way from Chaucer, Shakespeare, and Milton to Hemingway. She came from a wonderful family of evangelical stock steeped in Christian scholarship. Frances had about her a pristine quality, underscored by a measured and perfect spoken English. Her love for both her students and her Lord was contagious. Later, a faculty chair was inaugurated in her honor.

Unmarried during her time at Asbury, after accepting a teaching position at Taylor University in Upland, Indiana, she met her husband, Bill Ewbanks, a mathematician on the faculty. They were married for thirty years before their recent deaths. My wife, Rachel, and I count their friendship as one of our richest treasures.

I was also deeply impacted by the late Dr. Jim Young. He arrived on campus wearing a crew cut and so youthful looking he was mistaken by many of us as a fellow student. The first

A NEW CHALLENGE

week of school, I discovered that this young, presumed classmate was an esteemed and admired professor of speech and drama.

Though I had taken a speech class in high school, in this new and intimidating college setting, I experienced an unsettling terror as I approached my first assignment, a five-minute speech – five minutes that seemed like an eternity. That was the day I learned that "knees knocking" is not just a figure of speech. I almost forgot what my subject was in that terrible performance, but vividly recall, as I stammered my way through the delivery, that my knees truly were knocking, a phenomenon my fellow classmates were quick to observe. I calculated that this fiasco spelled the end of any ambition to be a public speaker, much less a preacher.

Jim too had a passion for his chosen field, and he knew how to encourage this love in others. By graduation, I had taken every one of his classes, both in speech and drama. Through the years, Rachel and I kept up our friendship with Jim and his wonderful wife, June. They also had a part in the support of our missionary work for more than forty years.

Z.T. Johnson, who had been Dad's classmate, was in his seventeenth year as president at Asbury. As an executive, Z.T. provoked decidedly mixed feelings. Without question, he was the man who, along with H.C. Morrison, had rescued the college from the brink of insolvency, wonderfully increased her enrollment, and guided her through the challenges following World War II. His name appears on two campus buildings.

But the mention of Z.T. Johnson did not always elicit feelings of warmth and affection. For many of us he was the most brusque, intimidating, and insensitive of all the school leaders. As class president of our Torchbearer class my junior year and the following year as student body president, I was required to talk with the man in his office, a sort of polar zone, not calculated to put anyone at ease. Later I was flabbergasted to learn that he had publicly commended me for my missionary service. Though I had met with Z.T. a number of times, he never gave any hint that he knew my father – his classmate – or that I existed. He always appeared totally distracted and would seem to count it a favor for me to make a hasty exit.

Chapter 10

A NEW COMPANION

My senior year witnessed innumerable changes. My two former roommates were gone. Grant was in Japan as a crusader. Earl was now married to Betty. That year I paid many visits to their small, rented apartment just off campus where I was warmly welcomed as a member of the family.

My new roommate was Stanley Lawrence. Stan was from Marion, Ohio, where his father and brother owned a large orchard and farm with a beautiful herd of Holstein cattle. The family had considerable property on the outskirts of Marion, and their great red barn adjacent to the highway was familiar to everyone in the area.

Stan took me home with him one weekend. His parents were stalwarts of the First Methodist Church and generous supporters. Stan's dad did his best to make me feel welcome. At mealtimes, this warm-hearted man and very savvy farmer heaped my plate shamelessly full of beef, potatoes, and all manner of delicious foods. When we returned to campus, they sent back with us a huge basket of apples from their orchard.

An added bonus was the fact that Stan had just been given a brand new baby-blue Ford Fairlane with the long flashy chrome "V" on either side and loaded with every imaginable accessory. Travel and double dates with Stan remain among my best memories of that year. Today Stan, a retired pastor, lives in Ohio. His wife, Karen, is a true helpmeet and they remain among our dearest friends.

Stan was the first to call my attention to a charming coed he had dated. Her name was Rachel Bright. She was a fellow Buckeye from Findlay, Ohio. "Ed," Stan said to me one evening, "I think you should date Rachel Bright. You would make a great couple." I had heard this kind of talk, dorm room chatter, before and was not inclined to give it much thought.

Curiously, however, another friend and classmate had similar ideas. His name was Jerry Symonds, and his father owned a farm equipment company on the outskirts of Findlay. Rachel and Jerry had been high school classmates. Now he approached me with the same opinion. "Ed," he said, "you have to date my friend. She is the perfect girl for you. How about I introduce you and set something up?" Then to top off his appeal, he said, "Her mother makes the best pecan pie I have ever eaten."

A short time later, Phil Falk, another friend who had also dated Rachel, approached me with the same notion. "Ed," he said, "you should date her. She is just the perfect girl for you." This was an interesting development. Three separate friends had come to me independently with the same strong conviction.

This notion, however, was altered to some degree by a conversation with an elderly man, George Slocum. His home was in Findlay where he had founded a Christian boys' club. Some of those boys were now students at Asbury, and George loved to come to campus to visit his former protégés. A confirmed bachelor, he was a frequent sight on Findlay's Main Street, sedately pedaling along on his old bicycle. George never owned a car nor ever learned to drive. To make his periodic journeys from Findlay to Wilmore, he had no qualms about bumming a ride with any student going his way.

Later, when he learned that I was dating Rachel, he showed concern. "Last week I rode with her down to campus," he said.

"Whew, you ought to see that girl drive. Talk about fast. I have never been so scared in my life!"

Rachel had entered Asbury as a freshman, although she was three years older than most of her classmates. After high school, she had taken a business course in Fort Wayne, Indiana, and then was employed as a secretary for two years at Marathon Oil headquarters in Findlay.

Her freshman year she was elected as a student council representative, which meant she would now sit on the council of which I was president. Though it was probably not love at first sight, there was without question a mutual attraction. The student body council generated more and more business, business that required long sessions with Rachel who was now the elected secretary.

We began dating, first a double date with roommate, Stan, and then supper and prayer meeting dates, leading to Monday afternoon walks on the campus. By the end of that first quarter, I was already categorizing Rachel as "my girl." Of course, I was delighted when she told me that God had called her to be a missionary.

Today, looking back on that senior year, I do find pleasure in several accomplishments. The first was a rewriting of the long-outdated student handbook. The second was the instituting of dormitory government with dorm students largely responsible for law and order. The third was that 1957 marked the inauguration of the college homecoming weekend, which afterwards was a regular feature of the school calendar.

My grades on the whole were acceptable but far from distinguished, unlike brother Bob who garnered a magna cum laude. I was not in the running for any academic honor. To my surprise at commencement, President Z.T. called Dad to come to the platform to present me with my diploma. Mom, Dad, Bob, and Vangie were in Wilmore, not only for my graduation but even more importantly to attend Bob and Phyllis's wedding, held in the seminary chapel that same afternoon.

During previous summers, following the end of the school year, I had headed directly for Yosemite. This year, with the flowering of my relationship with Rachel, we decided it was time for me to visit her home and become properly acquainted with her folks.

Rachel had grown up on a farm a few miles from Findlay. The Blanchard River runs through the town and was the inspiration for the folk song "Down By The Old Mill Stream." Rachel's ancestors had settled in the area after the War of 1812 and were at one time major landholders in Hancock County. In time, however, this land was divided among the many offspring, and her father, Ralph, ended up with enough to make a comfortable living for his wife and their four children.

Rachel's father, a gentle, unassuming man, was a farmer by necessity not choice. During his first year at Ohio State University, his father had died, and Ralph, as an only child, reluctantly returned home to run the farm. Thus, by this unfortunate turn of events, he had been forced into an occupation that was not his first choice. His wife, Inez Roller, was of hardy German stock, a woman of uncommon virtue and industry. Rachel's older sisters, Dorothy and Margaret, had both married outstanding gentlemen. Dorothy's husband, John, was a lawyer and for a time the mayor of Berea, a suburb of Cleveland, Ohio. Margaret's husband, Medford, was a prodigious worker and an outstanding farmer in their area near Mount Blanchard, Ohio.

Ironically, Rachel's brother, Eldon, was quite different from the girls in many ways. Gifted artistically, he studied at the Pittsburgh Art Institute where he was led to Christ by his roommate. When he came home, it was to insist that Rachel, despite her good character and perfect church attendance, needed to "get saved." This mandate coming from her brother did not initially set well with Rachel, but it was the first in a chain of events that led to a revival at the altar. That night the evangelist spoke words to her that proved to be prophetic. "Young lady," he said, "God may be calling you to be a missionary." Rachel felt led to get further education to prepare for whatever God wanted her to do.

At college that first year, Rachel began attending Student Volunteers, seeking to know God's will for her life. During a missionary conference, she had offered her life for missionary service.

Shortly thereafter, we began dating. I was an MK and had never wanted to do anything else but be a missionary.

All too soon, those blissful days at Findlay came to an end and I was once more headed for Camp Curry. This was my first summer in Yosemite without the companionship of my brother, who was now married and working in Lexington, while his wife, Phyllis, studied nursing. I missed Bob.

Our days of quarrelling and fierce competition were over, and we had learned to enjoy one another's company. More and more we discovered that we had almost everything in common: the India years in boarding school, the curious Woodstock culture, and our love for tennis and for books. Bob, a great reader, had won an annual prize at Woodstock for being the first to completely fill out his library card. Moreover, we had been together pastoring the Peoples Chapel that year.

I was not naturally the avid reader Bob was, but, in time, I developed a love for Westerns by Zane Grey and Luke Short, along with the African adventure tales of H. Ryder Haggard, especially *King Solomon's Mines* and *She*. As we matured, our interests broadened. I eventually almost entirely gave up fiction in favor of history and biography. To this day, Bob and I report to one another on recent books we have discovered and often exchange the volumes.

Growing up in an evangelical home with parents who almost exclusively read Christian literature, early on we began exploring the great world of Christian classics from Amy Carmichael and Andrew Murray to Hannah Whithall Smith. We also read missionary biographies, my favorite being *To the Golden Shore: The Life of Adoniram Judson* by Courtney Anderson.

Beyond our love for books, we shared a passion for sports and played many heated sets of tennis. In high school at Woodstock and later in college, we both made the track team and learned to shoot baskets, having rigged up a backboard on the side of our garage in Los Angeles. Another favorite sport was touch football. We became avid fans of USC and UCLA and developed an early loyalty to the Los Angeles Rams in the days of Bob Waterfield, Elroy "Crazy Legs" Hirsch, and "Deacon" Dan Towler. To these interests must be added our love for hiking, starting with overnight treks up into the mighty Himalayas and later the snowcapped Sierras.

During my second week at Yosemite that summer of 1957, I was seated on one of the giant log benches scattered along the walkways of Camp Curry. I was once again working in the dining room and waiting for the evening shift to begin. As I lazily surveyed the throng of tourists passing before me, a familiar face emerged – Bob's. My mouth fell open. What in the world was my brother doing here?

Following their wedding in early June, Phyllis was due back in nursing school at the University of Kentucky to complete her RN degree. Bob had landed a good-paying job on a local paint crew. In a disconsolate tone of voice, he explained how it was that he was once again in beautiful Yosemite Valley for the summer but now without his new bride.

The job in the paint company for some reason didn't pan out. "Since I was the newest employee," he explained, "I got laid off first. I decided that the smartest thing was to fly back for another summer at Camp Curry and try to get my old job back." "And leave your new bride?" I gasped. "How could you do that?" "I just didn't have much choice," he lamented. Bob moved into my tent, and I tried my best to offer companionship, but for him this was a new dispensation – married life. He was glum and greatly mournful, missing his new bride something fierce.

That summer I was in continual euphoria, reading Rachel's letters of encouragement and reflecting on the happy prospects of the coming school year. Bob's hangdog demeanor almost made me feel guilty. Then with three weeks of the Yosemite-employment summer remaining, Phyllis, out of nursing school for a month's break, took the bus to California and landed a job as a maid in the park. She and Bob were given a tent for married folk. The bliss of those last weeks, it appeared, more than made up for the interminable separation of June and July.

The last month of that summer has a special place in our memories, thanks to a visit from a quartet of dear friends from our OMS headquarters office in Los Angeles. Three of them had become true pals to us during my high school days. Unburdened by home and family responsibilities, they adopted us as younger brothers. They also frequently stayed with us when Dad was gone, and since Mom did not drive, they chauffeured Vangie and me to sundry appointments and errands, always with joy and laughter.

They were Cindy Williamson, later Dad's secretary; Vi Haines, a Canadian; and Evelyn Slusser, who always had a love for adventure, a hilarious sense of humor, and a penchant for practical jokes. On weekends, Evelyn volunteered to help with the youth in the local OMS Japanese Holiness Church.

With the office gals came my former roommate, Grant Nealis, who had recently returned from the crusade in Japan.

What a time we had! We picnicked at the beach and swam in the Merced River. All but one of the gang had brought a bathing suit. Since Evelyn had come from an ultra-conservative background, she had never owned a bathing suit. It was a shame to miss the fun. I finally coaxed her to get aboard a large air mattress, which we carefully guided to the middle of the river. "Oh, this is wonderful!" she enthused, just before the mattress accidentally-on-purpose upset. Screaming, she helplessly plunged into the cold water. Eventually she dried off and many years later called the experience the most "delightful surprise" of her life.

The following day we drove to Tuolumne Meadows, the high country fairyland that we so loved. There we strolled along the river that runs through the valley. We had brought our lunch and picnicked on one of the old bridges. For Bob and Phyllis, these days were the perfect substitute for the honeymoon that had been cut short.

CHAPTER 11

SEMINARY

That fall found me back at Asbury, no longer in college but across the street at Asbury Theological Seminary (ATS). The majority of Asbury College ministerial students were opting to take their seminary work at Emory University's Candler School of Theology in Atlanta. Because of an unfortunate development involving the dismissal of a professor, ATS had temporarily lost her accreditation.

It is still my view that in many ways the reduced student body was a blessing. Smaller classes fostered a family-like environment and increased interaction with godly professors. After all, Jesus' peripatetic school had an enrollment of only twelve.

Our beloved professor of evangelism, Robert Coleman, regularly took students out on the streets of Lexington on Saturday nights to witness. Professor J.T. Seamands, who had originally been an OMS missionary in India, was now professor of missions. For years, each summer he took students on mission trips to India.

Those of us who were unmarried seminarians enjoyed an especially intimate society as we all took meals together in the small dining room and lived in the confines of a couple of buildings. Many of these fellow students have been lifetime friends of mine.

Several of the former Every Creature Crusaders were now

pursuing their seminary studies with a view to return to the field as missionaries. Foremost among them was Grant Nealis. That year he married Dottie Bryant, a former missionary to Brazil, whom he had met earlier. They served in Hong Kong where Grant later became the OMS field director.

Other friends included a lanky blonde guy from Alabama, Austin Boggin, in my mind the quintessential evangelist always on the prowl for souls, and the big German-Canadian Helmut Schultz, whose parents had emigrated from Russia. He was in many respects the man I viewed as the perfect missionary. Full of the Spirit of God, he was known to agonize for nights in prayer.

In college, he had been elected president of Student Volunteers, and although he knew nothing of the finer points of chairing a business meeting, it didn't matter to him. He oozed love and always wanted to know how each person was doing spiritually. Added to this company of committed young men were Charles Dupree, Kelly Toth, and Stan Dyer.

My seminary roommate, a friend from college days, was Morris Holtzclaw from Crab Orchard, Kentucky. He had been saved as a GI in Japan, largely through the influence of Bob Boardman who was working with the newly organized Navigators. Morris and I were both ardently courting Asbury College girls and had marriage on our minds.

Morris had landed a two-point Methodist charge near a hamlet named Gravel Switch. Since I had terminated the Shelbyville pastorate, which remained under the administration of the college ministerial association, I agreed to accompany Morris on his weekly ministry at Gravel Switch. This meant working with the youth and occasionally preaching, which afforded no remuneration but great experience.

Morris was the perfect roommate, and we were always compatible. The only hitch in our relationship was the day I absentmindedly left the electric corn popper on and went to class. We returned to a scene of billowing black smoke, not only filling our room but also seeping out under the door into the long hallway. The odor of smoke, we soon learned, is not easy to remove from curtains and clothing!

During the first semester, I sensed in myself a kind of lethargy. Many of my college friends were now gone. I was tired of school, of classes. I had been in classrooms all of my life as far back as I could remember and was now facing another long three-year period in seminary. Beyond that, I was considering getting a master's degree in journalism. That would involve another year of study. A dull ennui I had never known before seemed to envelop me.

I entertained myself by drawing cartoons on various seminary-related subjects. These I tacked up in the dorm and occasionally on the large central bulletin board. One caricature showed Calvin and Wesley throwing mud at each other in a theological spat. Under the cartoon were the words: "People who get into mudslinging always lose ground."

Another cartoon I drew was about Dr. Turner's required Gospel of Mark class. George Turner, a lifetime advocate of the inductive study method, used charts in every class. He loved charts. This demanding Mark course was a requirement for all first-year students and, of course, a large complicated chart was required. Turner's devotion to charts was all too well known at ATS by both professors and students.

My cartoon depicted Mrs. Turner in the upper window of a house, now on fire and going up in smoke. Dr. Turner was holding the ladder for his wife who held a small child in her arms with flames shooting out on every side. To his wife's pleas to help save the child, Turner shouts, "No! No! The charts!" The cartoon was a big hit and sent peals of laughter through the classroom. My love for cartooning, which began as a child, has served me well and provided some lighter moments of mirth in life.

That winter John R. Church was the preacher at the college revival. This fervent evangelist was a fixture in many of the holiness camp meetings scattered throughout the central and southern United States. When he came to Asbury, Hughes Auditorium, which seats over a thousand, was packed every night to hear the great apostle. Both Morris and I loved the preaching of Dr. Church. We attended every evening service. In this pre-cassette era, Morris bought taped reels of his recorded messages. Again and again, we listened to his sermons in our room.

Rachel and I were now on different campuses and had different schedules. She, of course, was subject to the restrictive college social rules. This meant our time together required creative planning. Still, we managed to see a great deal of one another.

By fall, it was clear that both of us were thinking marriage, although the subject had not formally come up. Christmas break, which in those days lasted an entire month, provided an opportunity for a most strategic and important event. I had been to Rachel's home and met her family; now I determined that she must go home with me for Christmas.

Mom and Dad by this time could read pretty clearly my thoughts and plans concerning Rachel. If they had any objections, they did not voice them and, as they observed the two of us together, saw without question that "the fat was in the fire." That winter vacation in Los Angeles, although I continued to paint houses for OMS, I spent evenings with Rachel.

Strange to say, at this point and despite our romance, for the past several weeks my mind had been much occupied with thoughts of the OMS Every Creature Crusade, as a number of my friends were crusade veterans. The influence of these men had a telling effect upon me. Perhaps God also wanted me to taste the hardship and adversity of working in Asian villages for Christ. As I was increasingly drawn into the vortex of my love for Rachel, however, I reasoned that in two years, rather than being merely a two-year short-term crusader, I could be living on a field like India or Japan committed for an entire lifetime to faithful, zealous service for Christ.

Still, as the days passed, I found myself in a terrible dilemma. I determined that during the Christmas break I would seek Dad's counsel in the matter. I broached the subject one afternoon while we were alone. "Dad," I began, "I have been thinking a lot about the crusade and wondering if I should go."

After pondering the question for a moment, he said, "Well, as much in love as you and Rachel are, it might be better to marry, finish seminary, and then go to the field." Hallelujah! This was just the answer I had been hoping and praying for.

Dad's wisdom, in my mind, seemed to issue from Mount Olympus, and his counsel was on par with the Oracle of Delphi. Now, following Dad's counsel, I felt perfectly at ease, secure in my passionate desire for marriage, probably by the following summer. Dad's pronouncement had settled the issue, beyond question. A great sense of relief settled over me and with it a heavenly euphoria. I could hear wedding bells.

CHAPTER 12

ENGAGED

Back at Asbury, a most mischievous idea entered my mind. A nearby drug store had a gumball machine in the entryway. Among the gumballs were gaudy prizes to entice small children. This time, in response to the clank of my coin, out tumbled a ring, plastic of course, but covered with a dazzling façade of gold. Sitting atop the oval was what looked like the world's largest diamond.

The next Monday evening, after dinner with Rachel in the college cafeteria, I suggested that we go to a quiet corner of the basement of the administration building. We could be alone, and the chances of being observed by anyone else were remote. We sat down on an old bench. "Close your eyes," I whispered with a small mischievous smile. "Now hold out your hand." She complied. Onto her finger I now placed my newly acquired ring.

"Now," I softly instructed her, "you can open your eyes." As her eyes opened, she glimpsed the orgy of gold, topped off by a beautiful and enormous "diamond." Her eyes widened and her lips emitted a scream of delight. Halfway into this ecstatic response, however, she stopped, and a dark suspicion began to form.

To begin with, the amount of gold was far too large, too bright, and too extravagant. We had dated long enough for her to know my lifelong and habitual stinginess. In an instant, she blushed deep red. She clasped her face in her hands and shouted, "Oh, no, Ed! No, you couldn't! How could you do this to me?"

The only consolation at that moment came from the realization that after this shameful display, the real thing would surely be coming. That night came a few weeks later, a far less elaborate occasion than the event deserved. After dinner, we drove along a route familiar to many dating students, winding along bluegrass pastures, small farms with dark barns laden with drying tobacco. This brought us to High Bridge, which spanned the Kentucky River and was at one time the highest railroad bridge in the world. Just beyond were the premises of an old camp and tabernacle, now deserted. Beside the property was a large visitors' parking lot. No other car was in sight. I turned on some romantic music and slipped the ring – a pitifully small diamond, I might add – onto Rachel's finger. Clearly, the stone was a far cry from my original choice, but at least the band was gold and the tiny diamond was real.

This ring, I might add, was obtained from my now salesman friend, Helmut Schultz, who in a small way had entered the jewelry business in an effort to pay his college tuition. I have in recent years offered to replace Rachel's diamond with a larger one but she always refuses. "This one is fine and still in very good working order."

In the weeks that followed, while I floated along on velvet clouds, Rachel bent herself to the delightful task of planning the wedding. The date we finally agreed on was early in June. The venue would be the bride's home church. This was the First Evangelical United Brethren Church in Findlay, Ohio, constructed of brownstone and appropriately dignified for ceremonies such as weddings.

The first Tuesday in March, I was studying at my desk and in customary manner preparing the week's assignments. Suddenly the door flew open and our neighbor in an adjoining room entered, his face flushed with excitement. "Have you heard what's happened at the college?" he asked. I knew nothing of any unusual events across the street in our sister institution. "Revival has come!" he exclaimed. "It happened this morning during the chapel, just like the 1950 revival. It's still going on. Scores are at the altar and others lined up on the platform to give their testimonies. You must go over. See it for yourself."

I had a date with Rachel at noon, in exactly an hour. When I saw her, I would enquire about the so-called revival. At 11:55 a.m. I made my way across the street.

As I meandered over in the direction of the dining hall, I recall thinking it was strange that there were no couples or students of any kind lounging on the benches located on the shaded lawn that bordered the semicircle. I proceeded toward the entrance of the cafeteria, adjacent to Glide-Crawford Dorm where Rachel was housed. There was no evidence of any kind of student life. By lunchtime, there was always a line of students outside the building waiting to enter, but now not a living soul was in sight. I checked my watch. It was still running normally, the hand indicating exactly twelve o'clock. Strange, I pondered, very strange.

A sensation passed over me, harkening back to my childhood days in Allahabad, India. Upon awakening from an afternoon nap in our red brick bungalow, I discovered the house was entirely, unnaturally deserted. A tour of the bedrooms revealed that everyone was gone, not a soul was in sight, no human noises from any quarter.

Then the terrifying thought – It's happened! The Lord has come! The rapture has taken place. Mom, Dad, even Bob, have all been caught up. I'm the only one left. That Bob should have been taken and not me seemed quite beyond belief. Yet I knew, as oldsters frequently remark, there will be some big surprises when Christ returns.

While these thoughts were still being processed, my puzzlement deepened with the discovery that there were no students in the cafeteria. I glanced through the large entryway to the kitchen. It was deserted.

Still trying to unravel the mystery, I then recalled the report of the morning, words I had so summarily dismissed. Could it be that our neighbor was right? The great revival of which he spoke had come? I headed towards Hughes Auditorium at the other end of the semicircle. As I moved along the walkway past the administration building with its high steeple, I caught unusual sounds issuing from the auditorium, faintly at first, then murmurs of human voices in a gentle cacophony, unlike anything I had ever heard before in my years of weekly gatherings in that historic auditorium.

Now what I heard was not the usual amens and hallelujahs in response to warm-hearted preaching, nor was it the senatorial voice of a pulpit orator of the sort often invited to fill Asbury's pulpit. Nor was it a great chorus of music, the huge pipe organ and happy harmony of human voices raised in joyful hymns or the beloved gospel songs of the church. No, nothing like that.

There came to my mind a verse from St. John's revelation of heaven, which compares the cries of the saints to the sound of many waters. Yes, that was it, a sort of chorus of human voices, some raised in joy joined with others full of petitions and all varieties of human cries.

I had worshiped in Hughes regularly for more than three years, since college rules require attendance at the thrice-weekly chapel services. The sacred environs of that hall draw the eye to focus on the stately gold-colored organ pipes across which are inscribed the words "Holiness Unto the Lord." This scene remains in the mind of alumni, a veritable Bethel, Peniel, or Mount of Transfiguration – sacred soil where we had met God and come away forever altered.

Passing through the door, I was confronted by a sight unlike anything I had ever witnessed. Hundreds were kneeling at their seats. In front, others were kneeling along the polished wooden altar, two-, three-, and four-deep. Some sat quietly transfixed with faces bowed or raised heavenward, some streaked with tears, others transfigured by heavenly light and unearthly joy.

For most, however, their gaze was fixed on the large pulpit on the platform. One student was speaking and behind him a row of his fellow students stretched the length of the platform and down to the aisle below. All were waiting to give testimony, desperately eager to tell what God had done for them.

This heavenly outpouring, I learned, had started during the morning chapel service, when the president of the senior class had asked that, prior to the regularly scheduled message, he be permitted to say a few words. What followed was a tearful recital as the young man described how he had been a great pretender, making eloquent profession of faith while all the while living a lie. "I'm going to the altar right now," he announced, "and I will stay there till God has met my need."

At Asbury, since its inception, such unscheduled interruptions, resulting in students humbling themselves before God and man, had been viewed as sacred events. Almost immediately, others rose from their seats to join the young man. The floodgates of heaven, it seemed, had been thrown open, the floodtides of divine power unleashed. Some of those present, particularly the faculty who had witnessed the phenomenon of the 1950 revival, recognized that this present unfolding drama had all the marks of authenticity.

By noon, when I entered the auditorium, the cataract of blessing had been flowing for about three hours. As word of revival circulated, a gradually increasing stream of people began arriving on campus. Local radio and TV reporters showed up to interview Asbury students and faculty. All classes in the college were suspended. By evening of that first day, news of these happenings had spread throughout the United States and even to foreign countries.

I found a seat toward the rear of Hughes and sat there terribly sober and, I confess, increasingly uneasy. I took a break for supper at the seminary dining hall. All around me, sober voices spoke of nothing other than the events across the street.

That evening I still had not seen Rachel and was back at Hughes Auditorium sitting alone toward the rear. I admitted to myself with some guilt that my initial response to the wonderful event was anything but enthusiastic. In fact, I told myself that the divine outpouring had come at a most inconvenient time. Not only were Rachel and I in the middle of wedding plans, but the following week were mid-term exams. My conscience immediately rebuked me for such impious thoughts. I should be entering into the spirit of the revival with unrestrained joy and excitement, but I knew all too well how these unfolding events could wreak havoc with our upcoming plans.

During the following hours as testimonies and cries of victory resounded through the night and into the early morning, there came upon me a terrible heaviness. My mind was riveted on the events of recent months, and at the same time, I had a growing conviction that God was indeed calling me to join the Every Creature Crusade prior to my marriage to Rachel. These thoughts I quickly sought to dismiss. It was, I told myself, all some kind of psychological phenomenon, perhaps the work of the Devil in his effort to interrupt our sacred union. I would put it behind me and get a good night's rest. I would be fine in the morning. After all, had not Dad, a man so singularly wise and spiritual, advised me to marry first and then go to the mission field? My tortuous thoughts, I told myself, were a sort of perverse autosuggestion that would pass by morning.

The revival, instead of diminishing and coming to a joyous

and happy close, having satisfied the demands and purposes of the Spirit, was in fact gathering momentum. The following week, services were moved to the Methodist church, a block off campus. The sanctuary was packed every night, the altar filled. Though I faithfully attended the services, for my tortured heart there was no rest. The long night hours were mostly bereft of slumber, my thoughts and mind engaged in an endless warfare against divine intimations.

Studying for upcoming mid-terms was futile. I was completely incapable of concentrating on anything other than God's persistent call. Then came a voice that insisted, "God will not approve anything short of His intractable will." This surrender, I knew, meant postponing our wedding for two and a half years so I could join the crusade in Asia.

Now I discovered a phenomenon I had previously known but never truly experienced. When one is determined to follow his own schemes and live out the plan he has set his heart on, he will become aware of an annoying fact: Scriptures learned even as a child will "turn on him." The psalmist knew this when he wrote: *Wherewithal shall a young man cleanse his way? by taking heed thereto according to thy word* (KJV).

Three Scriptures particularly assailed me. My thoughts were infuriatingly drawn repeatedly to 1 Samuel 15:22 and the words *To obey is better than sacrifice* (KJV). Like the rebellious King Saul, I was offering sacrificial gifts to Him while insisting on my own plans.

The second Scripture was Christ's piercing words to Simon Peter at Galilee after His resurrection as recorded in John 21:15: *Simon, son of Jonas, lovest thou me?* (KJV) This question cut like a knife in my heart. I was perfectly certain that the same question, spoken now to my stubborn heart, could only refer to our wedding plans.

One more verse repeatedly came to mind. In Acts 26 where

Paul's testimony is recorded, Christ addresses him: *Saul, Saul, why do you persecute me? It is hard for you to kick against the goads.* Then the Spirit whispered to me, "Going against my will is to choose the spikes of God's goad." This was not a pleasant thought.

These were terrible days for me. The effusive sentiment of romance had evaporated; the anticipated bliss had vanished. Another Scripture that I hardly realized I knew came to mind. The words of David in the Psalms: *For day and night thy hand was heavy upon me* (KJV).

The first step of surrender came on the heels of a terrifying thought voiced by a dear woman, who in her youth had been clearly and wonderfully called to be a missionary. At the time, however, she was deeply in love and the wedding was planned. She was to marry a distinguished man – wealthy, handsome, kind, generous, and one who loved her deeply. But he was not a Christian. With tears, I heard again her plea to the youth in a large congregation. "Young people," she pled, "you can have everything you ever wanted and every dream come true, but then find out you can never be truly happy outside the will of God." And then she went on with this sober question: "Do you know what it means to get up every morning with the realization that you have missed God's best for your life?"

I had recently read of the life of Hudson Taylor. In the book were his favorite words with respect to God's will: "Enough that God my Father knows: nothing this faith can dim. He gives the very best to those who leave the choice with Him." His call, which appears to be an impossible sacrifice, is really an unspeakable blessing in disguise.

Then I gradually realized that God who was dealing so harshly with me was preparing for me a gift wonderful beyond imagination. Somewhere in Asia, I told myself, there are people in stygian darkness and ignorance who have waited a lifetime for the divine light, and God has determined that I should be for them the bearer of that light.

That night I said an agonizing final yes. "Lord, I know this is your call, and I choose to live in the center of your will and purpose. As for the crusade in Asia, my answer is yes. I will do as you ask and leave the consequences with you."

A great peace enveloped me, peace like no other, a sweet electric current moving down from my brain into my arms and fingers, into every molecule of my being. I thought of a line from a gospel song: "There is sunshine in my soul today, more glorious and bright."

Then came a sudden consternation. How in the world will I tell Rachel?

The next day, I had a luncheon appointment with Rachel at the college cafeteria. In the intervening hours as I anticipated the fateful meeting, I prayed that somehow she would be of a suitable frame of mind to receive the outrageous news I would be bringing. Perhaps the Lord had already intimated to her something of my struggle. Possibly, she too for some reason was considering delaying our nuptials.

When I met her at 11:45 a.m., it was immediately apparent that no such presentiments had prepared her in any way for the meeting. It was just the opposite, in fact. She had exciting news for me. That morning she had been to Lexington. A gorgeous wedding gown that had earlier caught her eye was the one she had decided on. In a transport of rapture, she proceeded to describe the garment in every detail – the material, the lace, the length, the cut, the train, and even the veil. In the midst of this recital, she sensed that I was not sharing her excitement. Before the recital had ended I broke in, "Rachel, there is something that I need to tell you."

Now she could tell from my somber, tortured expression and the fitful way in which I searched for words to express my thoughts, that the news I was about to share would not delight her. Finally, I managed to get out, "Well, what I am trying to say is that God is calling me to join the crusade."

"You mean a few months and then we can be married."

"No, not a few months, but over two years; that is how long the crusade term lasts."

"Two years?" she echoed with alarm. "That's a long time and I've already bought my dress and what will my parents say?"

I had already anticipated these questions and now struggled for words. Two and a half years was to our minds, indeed, a small eternity. What could happen in that stretch of time? Rachel had had plenty of other suitors. Would she really wait for me that long, be faithful to me, and forego a social life all that time? Satan whispered that this was unlikely and, even if she did wait, there was no guarantee that I would return. Asia at the time, after World War II, was an impoverished and a most unhealthy place to live, especially in villages lacking many of the basics of sanitation and hygiene.

"I know this is terrible," I went on, "and so unfair to you, but I can't escape the terrible conviction that this is God's will for me. I feel it so deeply that I can't sleep, can't eat, can't study. I feel that if I don't yield to His call, I will die."

Rachel responded with "This isn't right. This can't be God's will because the Scriptures say, *Let all things be done decently and in order*, and this isn't decent or in order."

I continued. "I just want you to do one thing – pray about this. I will too, and then tomorrow afternoon at two o'clock let's meet at the prayer chapel."

After a pause, she agreed. "Okay," she said, looking forlorn and deeply troubled. "I'll meet you there."

Early the following afternoon, I met Rachel at the agreed-upon hour. Together we walked to the prayer chapel, actually the first building of Asbury College. The ground floor originally housed the classrooms, the second floor a dormitory for the small student body consisting of about thirty students. The lower floor had been converted into a museum. Above was the prayer chapel, a favorite rendezvous for devout couples and some not so devout but intent on a few minutes of privacy, safe from the inquiring eyes of the campus security guards or watchmen.

It was to this sacred shrine we resorted that March afternoon in 1958. We walked up the stairs in silence. Situated on the kneeling cushion at the foot of the altar, Rachel broke the silence. "Ed, I've been praying, and we really don't have any choice. If God is asking us to do this, postpone our marriage for two and a half years while you go to the crusade, we have to do it. I will complete my studies while you are gone."

When we finished praying, I noticed a large pulpit Bible lying open on top of the altar. This was one of those ponderous tomes, also intended to serve as a family record of births and marriages over several generations. I noticed now that the book had been left open to John 15, a very familiar chapter to me. I had studied it in high school at Culter, and Dr. Hanke, who taught New Testament at Asbury, required the students of the sophomore Bible class to memorize the entire chapter, which I had done.

I began reading through the familiar passage. *I am the vine; you are the branches.* Then suddenly we came to verse 16, the reading of which brought to me a sudden and strange sensation. It was as though I had never seen it before and it was written just for me. *You did not choose me, but I chose you.* I paused and acknowledged the truth, now alive with new meaning. Then I went on: *so that you might go.* That's what Jesus had said. *Go into all the world and preach the gospel.* How could any verse in the Bible be more suited to our situation?

The next few words were a promise: *bear fruit – fruit that will last.* Growing up on a foreign field, I knew that there is a great deal of so-called fruit that never lasts. Then, as though to answer a secret, unspoken terror that stemmed from the fact that all OMS missionaries were required to raise their support, I received an incredibly comforting answer: *and so that whatever you ask in my name the Father will give you.* I sat there feeling like Saul en route to Damascus. I had not only seen the light, but had heard the voice of God.

Looking back on that afternoon in 1958 from this perspective of more than half a century later, I am still profoundly moved by His patience and tender grace poured out upon one so insistent on his own will. I have come to regard that day as a sort of continental divide so deeply altering my pilgrim journey that thereafter I could never be quite the same.

In John 12, our Savior said, *Unless a kernel of wheat falls to the ground and dies, it remains only a single seed. But if it dies, it produces many seeds* (KJV). To gain such fruit, I now understood, required a kind of dying. This same shocking fact is often repeated. *If any man will come after me, let him deny himself, and take up his cross* – a symbol of death.

This sacrifice, I am fully convinced, left me a very different person, changed in many ways. This too I believe was a sort of necessary experience God demanded for a breakthrough to a new dimension in my spiritual journey. How strange that such pain could open the heart's door to unspeakable bliss.

I now felt a new freedom in preaching. With full courage and sincerity, I could urge people to taste the sweetness of God's perfect will in their lives and enter into the adventure of full abandonment to the will of God. My love for Scripture I trace back to my sophomore year in high school when I vowed to spend time every day in God's Word. I regularly repeated to myself Jeremiah 15:16: *Thy words were found, and I did eat them; and thy word was unto me the joy and rejoicing of mine heart* (KJV). In many ways, the Bible became a new book, not only to be read but also memorized and pondered in meditation day and night.

Besides the Scriptures, I now craved all manner of Christian books, particularly devotional classics which shed light on the Bible and the deeper life. Memorization, particularly of the Psalms, became an inexpressible delight. My favorite at this time was Psalm 16:11: *In thy presence is fullness of joy; at thy right hand there are pleasures for evermore* (KJV).

Since all of the crusaders in the second Every Creature Crusade had been dispatched to Japan, I naturally assumed that I too would spend my term in that land. As it happened, however, the very week OMS received my letter offering myself for the crusade, my parents were in Taiwan, then known as Formosa, and staying with dear friends Rolland and Mildred Rice. The field committee had met with Dad to discuss and agree on launching the Every Creature Crusade in Taiwan. The next day they learned of my application to OMS to join the crusade. Immediately, Rolland Rice called a field committee meeting and entered an official minute inviting me to serve in Taiwan.

This sequence of events from the outset seemed strangely and wonderfully providential and proved more and more so with the passage of time. Since my initial call had been to the crusade and not necessarily to Japan, my heart was at peace. I promptly informed OMS and the Taiwan field that I would accept their invitation. I still have a copy of my old crusade prayer card with my picture on it. I see there an incredibly young man in a checkered blue sports coat. At the bottom, I am classified as a crusader and in large letters running down the side of the card is the word "Formosa."

CHAPTER 13

FUNDING

In the wake of my commitment to join the crusade came the very intimidating issue of funding, raising my own support which all OMS missionaries, both overseas and homeland, were required to do. They accomplished this, for the most part, by inviting friends and churches to take one or more shares in their support, a share being a faith promise of $5 a month.

Now OMS informed me that I would be required to raise thirty $5-per-month shares before my departure scheduled for August of that year. The sum by today's standards was miniscule, amounting to $150 a month as my allowance and additional cash for transportation to and from the field. How could I raise this money? Unlike most crusaders, since I had lived abroad most of my life, I had no home church or large body of friends to whom I could appeal.

A couple of weeks later I got a call from Larry Burr, the executive secretary of the newly formed Men for Missions, a laymen's ministry within OMS founded by Dwight Ferguson. Larry was holding weekend meetings in Virginia. Would I like to go along and give my testimony? Grant Nealis would also be going. Here was my first funding opportunity, and I would be comfortable with OMS friends.

Our destination was a small, rural Methodist church in Virginia, pastored by Asburians Carl and Dottie Crowe. They were unpretentious, warm-hearted folk who loved Christ and overflowed with southern hospitality.

In the weekend services, I was asked to give my testimony. I began nervously but then with increasing fervor as I described the length to which God had gone to change my wedding plans and persuade me to join ECC. By the time we started home on Monday, I had my first few shares. God had given me my first fruit, with the promise that the rest would come in His time.

My next meeting came by invitation of my former roommate, Earl Andrews, now pastoring a small church on the outskirts of Cincinnati. I preached and presented my share needs, and then in the evening I challenged the youth to offer themselves to God for Christian service and missions. The altar was lined with kneeling high schoolers, some praying for salvation, others answering God's call to ministry. As he had been in Shelbyville, Earl was warmly appreciated by everyone. After his plea for my needs, the shares came in, largely, I think, on the strength of the people's love for their pastor.

Two things about that weekend remain clear in my memory today after more than fifty years. An elderly lady church member, an immigrant from Scotland, told me one of the most remarkable stories I have ever heard.

As a small child, she had been extremely ill and then pronounced dead by a physician. Caskets in those days in Scotland often had a glass cover to enable friends to view the deceased at the funeral without risk of offensive odor. At the graveside, just as the casket was about to be lowered into the grave, someone noticed that a slight mist had gathered on the glass directly above her head. A halt was called to the ceremony and the glass removed. Incredibly, the girl was still alive and would live to her eighties, entertaining many friends and acquaintances with her Ripley's *Believe It or Not!* story.

The second anecdote is a sad illustration of the Scripture

that tells us that we are known by our deeds. One of the most verbal and flamboyant members of that little church was a good-looking and apparently confident gentleman who was also the church pianist. Caught up in the excitement of helping serve Christ in foreign lands, our pianist friend publicly pledged not one but two shares to me. In totaling up the offering and shares, Earl remarked, "If I were you, I wouldn't count on the two shares from the pianist." When I inquired the reason for this pronouncement, Earl gave me a wry smile. "He is one of those people who talks big, promises a lot, but I've never known him to follow through on anything. This is especially true where money is involved."

More sanguine than Earl, I was inclined to believe that the matter of these two precious shares, which I very much needed, would be repeatedly brought to the young man's mind, making it impossible for him to be delinquent in this matter. In the following two years, every month I examined my list of givers but our brother's name never appeared on any of them.

At the end of the 1957-58 school year, my first in seminary, I had spent a week with Rachel at her home. The next week Dad arrived. We had agreed that I would accompany him that summer on a swing through the southern states, visiting mission constituents and one in particular. The aging widow of a Methodist minister in Florida had informed OMS that she had a rather large gift for the mission, one that could not be mailed but required personal receipt by an authorized mission representative. It was a lovely and companionable drive south with Dad during those pre-interstate days.

I had previously traveled with Dad on deputation tours to camp meetings. It was always my task to move among the people and pass out our official OMS magazine, the *Missionary Standard* (now *OMS Outreach*).

Possibly my best conversations with Dad were on those long

drives. He would speak of his childhood exploits on the ball fields in Racine, Wisconsin, and later in the Chicago suburb of Austin where he had spent his teenage years. Enamored of the stars of his day, he had worn his cap at the same angle as Honus Wagner did, and as a lad, he had actually seen both Ty Cobb and Babe Ruth play.

We stopped briefly at Silver Springs, but Dad viewed a cruise for the two of us in the famed glass-bottomed boats an unnecessary extravagance. Our family's OMS salary was two hundred dollars a month since Mother also worked at the headquarters as editor of the mission magazine. We counted our change, often quite literally.

Twice during high school I had loaned my father money to buy seat covers for the car. In my junior year in high school, Dad decided that it would be acceptable for OMSers to own a television set. I took seventy-five dollars from my savings, enough to buy the family a used set. Though not initially in favor of TV, Dad, we were later to discover, had taken a liking to Perry Mason and when home would watch the show nearly every week.

There were few motel chains in 1958, no Holiday Inns or Days Inns. Tourist homes still did a good business, and it was to these establishments that we resorted in the evenings. When we arrived in Florida, we located the minister's widow who lived in a small frame house in a lower-class neighborhood. Dad introduced himself, and she immediately recognized him as the face she saw every month on the editorial page of the OMS magazine.

One remarkable impression of the home that remains in my memory was that, upon entering, we were greeted by stacks and stacks of paperback novels, mostly mysteries. That a devout minister's widow, one who was now intent upon giving OMS a large sum of money, was pre-occupied with something less than Christian literature was quite a shock to me.

The woman led the two of us into the bedroom and indicated that if the back wall of the clothes closet were removed we would discover a considerable sum of money. Since the Great Depression, the woman had lost confidence in banks and most of her savings was in that hide-away in the form of silver, boxes and boxes of silver – nickels, dimes, quarters, fifty-cent pieces, and even silver dollars.

Dad was glad that I had come along to lift these heavy "burdens." The woman had advised her bank that a great cache of silver was being delivered to Dr. Erny and advised them to prepare for the receipt of the treasure. Once our car was loaded with the precious boxes, we drove to the local bank and left with a check for the total amount. Our mission was accomplished.

We now headed north to our next destination, Winona Lake, Indiana, and the OMS annual conference. This was the single biggest and most important event in the mission's calendar year and usually was scheduled for the first week of July. It always started on Monday evening and concluded on Sunday afternoon.

That summer of 1958 there were about a dozen crusaders, either coming or going, at the convention. Those of us who were departing tried to glean from the veterans pertinent information relative to the adventure upon which we were about to embark. We assisted in the youth services and also gave our testimonies in the various rallies throughout the day. Among these 1958 candidates was Kemp Edwards, a fellow Asburian a year behind me. He too had been present during the great spring revival, which inspired him to offer himself to OMS for the crusade. Kemp later joined me in summer deputation, and we traveled together by ship to Asia.

On Thursday afternoon, Dale Neff, recently returned from Japan, called a meeting of all us crusaders attending the convention. He proposed that we spend a night in prayer for the concluding sessions of the convention, especially focusing on Friday's youth night when young people in attendance would be challenged to give themselves to God for foreign missions.

I had read of folks who spent entire nights in prayer but had never personally attempted such a thing. I rather supposed that these feats were accomplished by rare super saints, quite beyond the status of ordinary Christians such as me. Nevertheless, I showed up at the appointed hour after the close of the evening service.

About eight of us were there with Dale taking the lead. The fervor occasioned by the evening meeting and events of the day kept us going well past midnight. By then some of us were fighting drowsiness and were troubled by sore knees. In long prayer vigils, there's a phenomenon akin to the marathoner's second wind, which follows the proverbial "hitting the wall." In the early hours of the morning, we got our second wind.

Prayers now seemed at times to gush forth in a cataract of intercession, pouring out almost as though unbidden, a torrent of petitions accompanied by sensations of great liberty and joy, continuing until the purple dawn signaled the start of a new day. Though later in my life there were other all-night prayer meetings, that first one was one which none of us, now old crusaders, will ever forget.

Dad, the one who envisioned and organized the second crusade, rejoiced to see a number of new prospective candidates kneeling at the altar almost every night. He always took charge of the conventions, making sure that the financial needs of outgoing missionaries, especially crusaders, were presented. The result was that by Saturday afternoon, almost all of us had garnered the required number of shares.

After the convention, Kemp and I had several meetings as we began the long drive to Los Angeles and the OMS headquarters.

FUNDING

Long hours with a companion, driving halfway across the vastness of America, provided a unique opportunity for getting to know one another very well. Kemp had a great baritone voice, and I prevailed upon him to sing solos in all of our meetings.

Every morning, Kemp ordered biscuits for breakfast at local restaurants with special instructions to the waitress. Kemp would cajole and plead with the waitress not to bring the biscuits until they were truly done. Whatever the poor woman did to them, they never quite measured up to his standard. Finally, in frustration, Kemp would plead, "Tell the chef to make them well done, brown, dark, burnt." Since I had grown up on meager fare in boarding school where we were happy just to have sufficient food, regardless of the quality, I became increasingly frustrated by these little biscuit dramas each morning.

Many years later, I was in west Texas interviewing our inveterate "dentist" missionary, Nobie Pope. She had pulled thousands of teeth from the mouths of suffering Indians along the Magdalena River in Colombia, South America. Nobie loved biscuits and, in the mornings before I interviewed her, she would have a fresh batch in the oven.

One morning, she was so totally absorbed in our work that she forgot the biscuits. Presently we smelled the alarming odor of something burning. Then came billows of dark smoke emerging from the kitchen. Nobie jumped to her feet shouting, "It's my biscuits! I forgot them!" She rushed into the kitchen but it was too late, much too late. "Don't throw those biscuits away, Nobie," I pled. "I want them!" Three days later Kemp received in the mail my gift with a note reading: "I finally found biscuits well done enough for even you."

In Louisville, we picked up Route 150 and then drove along the river to St. Louis and Route 66, which took us through Missouri, Oklahoma, Texas, New Mexico, and Arizona. In Kansas, we were guests of a former classmate at Asbury, now the pastor of a small Methodist church. He had planned a fishing expedition for us. In preparation, we wandered through the fields collecting live grasshoppers, a favorite meal for the succulent catfish.

In Albuquerque, New Mexico, we had been invited to spend a weekend and preach in a church there. Years later while in Taiwan, I received a letter from South America. I did not recognize either the name or the address. The sender wrote, "I wonder if you remember the Sunday you preached in our church. I wanted you to know that I went to the altar answering God's call to be a missionary. Today my wife and I are serving the Lord in Brazil."

Though much of the time we do not know the end result of the seed we sow and will not until we get to heaven, yet now and then God allows us a glimpse of how He has used us. This is always a great encouragement, often coming at a time when we most need it.

Continuing our journey to the West Coast, we passed through the familiar desert towns, the final markers on the long journey to Los Angeles. In Arizona, we toured the Grand Canyon and the Petrified Forest. Near the California border at Gila Bend, temperatures often soar to 115 degrees. We usually timed our trip to arrive at Needles, this outpost on the border of the Mojave Desert, late in the evening so as to traverse the desert at night. Of course, in those days without air conditioning, when Mother made that trip, she insisted that before starting the desert drive we buy a block of ice to fend off the fierce desert heat.

This final stretch is redolent with memories. The Pasadena Freeway merges into the Hollywood Freeway at old Chinatown, a favorite haunt of OMS missionaries who knew where to get a six-course Chinese dinner for eighty-eight cents and, as the saying went, "with six you get egg roll." Those were the old days when Los Angeles was still a comparatively small city, smaller than Philadelphia with a population of less than two million.

It was good to be back at OMS headquarters at what was referred to as the Hilltop, a few acres of elevated land at the corner of North Hobart and Lemon Grove. Being here always brought waves of happy sentiment, the comfort and joy that poets celebrate as "Home Sweet Home."

During my high school and college days, Dad's travels, usually to the eastern states where the bulk of our constituency was located, kept him away from home an average of six months a year. In my four years of high school and participation in varsity sports, I recall Dad attending one of my football games, one basketball game, one baseball game, and one track meet. Dad was without question my great hero. It never occurred to me to feel resentment because he was almost always gone.

The weeks Dad was home, struggling to catch up on great piles of correspondence, paperwork, and committee matters all awaiting his return, he always found time for us. Except in cases of dire emergency, he spent evenings at home, relaxing with the family. He seldom brought office work home. I had fixed a basket to the side of our garage, and on Saturday afternoons, Dad often joined me in shooting baskets.

In our home I never heard Mother complain about his long absences and the inconvenience of having to raise children practically alone or being dependent upon others for transportation. There was always a note of pride and joy in her voice when she talked animatedly of Eugene's ministry and the marvelous things that God was doing around the world through OMS.

Now, however, I was aware of a subtle change in my status. Back at the hub of the mission, I was no longer just one of the Erny boys, but was a missionary in my own right. It was a curious and not an altogether pleasant sensation.

Home had been for many years the place to come for holidays

and fun. Now the pattern had changed. The boy had grown up and in his place now stood a missionary. Before, it was always missions by birth. I could not be held responsible for that – a good thing, all right, but not my obligation. Now it was missions by choice, no longer accidental or incidental.

At this time, however, I was becoming aware of Mother's serious health concerns. Being in her fifties marked the beginning of a travail that I could not at the time understand or appreciate. Her position as wife of the Mission president, as well as editor of the *Missionary Standard,* brought with it a load of work and social responsibilities that resulted in considerable stress.

Grandmother Helsby too had in midlife experienced terrible health problems, several major surgeries, and depression so severe that at times the children were placed in the homes of neighbors. Now it seemed the same dark malady was settling on Mother, a depression so deep that it would eventually require hospitalization, shock treatments, and dependence on anti-depressants, which in those days had troubling side effects.

Coming home from college for Christmas holidays, I had little idea of the "slough of despond" into which Mother had descended. She spent hours in bed and, when Dad was away, depended on the ministrations of dear OMS colleagues for comfort. I recall my bewilderment one year when I arrived home to find Mother in perpetual tears. She would pull me onto the bed beside her, agonizing, "Sit with me, Ed, sit with me. Pray with me. It is dark, so dark." It would be long years before I would in my own travail have any idea of what Mother was suffering.

Chapter 14

SPIRITUAL INSIGHTS

As I prepared to leave for Formosa, I recalled the words of Hudson Taylor, founder of the China Inland Mission (now OMF International), who wrote:

Well do I remember, as in unreserved consecration I put myself, my life, my friends, my all upon the altar. A deep solemnity came over my soul, the assurance that my offering was accepted. The presence of God became unutterably real and blessed. For what service I was accepted I did not know but a deep consciousness that I was no longer my own took possession of me, which has never since left me. Within a few months of this time of consecration, the impression came into my soul that the Lord wanted me in China.

I too found myself called to China and the province of Formosa, which was now the Republic of China. A great aid in obedience is to have forebears who have established certain family values, foremost of which is a headlong, unreserved commitment to do the full will of God without conditions or reservations. It was our privilege to know in Taiwan three generations of the Hudson Taylor family, all of whom, like their famous ancestor, had given themselves to God to reach the nations for Jesus Christ.

I now struggled to analyze the profound changes in my life since that spring of 1958. Words fail in my attempt to describe the process by which God worked His will in my life. To begin with, it brought profound insight into the matter of revelation. God not only spoke to prophets and saints in the distant past; He can and does speak with terrible force and clarity today. Since my conversion at an early age, I had known quite often a sweet comfort and sense of God's presence, and from my daily reading of His Word, I had gained instruction and holy intimacy. Now I had experienced a dogged and insistent voice in the night, refusing to be silent, insisting that this timid soul do the improbable, the impossible.

This was something new. In a letter I received from my brother, Bob, he asked if, in my thinking, this experience was in fact sanctification, a filling of the Holy Spirit. I did not define it as such. In my first year at Pasadena Nazarene College, I had battled for some time with the doctrine of a second work of grace subsequent to salvation. I had attended an excellent Christian high school in Los Angeles, staffed by godly folk who, I think, believed that holiness and empowerment came through sedulous Christian discipline, growth, and "walking in the light," not a second crisis. The filling of the Holy Spirit was not a phrase they would have used in this context, but then God is not overly concerned with vocabulary.

During the fall revival at Pasadena Nazarene, I went to the altar to humble myself (a needful act) and pray for what they chose to call entire sanctification. There followed a blessed peace and an inner insurance that now I was indeed filled with God's Spirit. However, with that experience, there was no great cost involved, no deep dying, and no flinging of myself with abandon into the unknown and seemingly perilous will of God.

Now I wrote to Bob saying, "I feel that the spiritual landscape of my life has radically changed." This was accompanied by several powerful new affections. The first was prayer, which in the past had been more duty than delight. There came a new intimacy in prayer, a fresh passion that I had not previously known. With the surrender of my beloved bride for an "eternity" of two years, the bridal chamber was occupied and fragrant now with the presence of Jesus himself and His comforting, instructing, encouraging, and enabling Spirit. This phenomenon or pattern is regularly found in the lives of saints who sacrifice marriage for divine calling.

Moreover, God's Word, which I had always loved and memorized from childhood, now became a passion. In my journal, I wrote these words:

> God, help me to understand the imperative of your Word because: (1) you have promised to bless not man's word but your holy Word; (2) every man of God has been characterized by an insatiable love for the Book; (3) the Bible has always had its rightful and prominent place in revival, both in individuals and in the church; (4) it is my daily sustenance; (5) it is the source of my instruction; (6) it is the sword of the Holy Spirit in witnessing; (7) it is the immovable fortress in the hour of temptation; (8) it provides an answer to every situation I encounter; (9) and it is an unfailing source of guidance.

I would like to report that this new fervor for both prayer and Bible study has remained constant throughout my life, but alas, this is not the case. Since communion with God and His Son through the Word and conversation – prayer – is in reality the Christian lifeline, it is therefore the very discipline that Satan targets first. It is his primary point of attack and must be guarded above all.

I am comforted in reading the biographies of saints, Christian heroes, who frequently admit struggles in this very area. Saint Teresa of Avila, great woman of prayer that she was, at times felt that her devotion had become a weariness and a bore. Once in reference to the quiet hours, she wrote, "Thank goodness that is done for the day." Still, as we mature, we learn so well that time alone with God is a great essential for peace, power, and perseverance. The sacred hour is the bastion and fortress of the soul.

There are two familiar metaphors I use to reflect on this earthquake in the landscape of my spiritual pilgrimage. The first is a kind of crossing of the Rubicon where I sensed a point of do or die, of complete obedience or the prospect of a life of mediocrity. It was the point of no return, an abandonment of self to God forever, come what may. The second metaphor is the continental divide. So changed was the environment of my soul that after that terrible, glorious spring, I've unconsciously categorized my life as "before '58 and after '58."

As my time in the U.S. was coming to a close, I was obliged before departing to settle financial accounts with the mission. This sort of chore has always proved a trial. I spent the good part of a day trying to untangle my much-mangled accounts. All summer long, I had been making out meeting reports incorrectly. The result was that now everything was a mess. I was not exactly sure that I had raised enough money for my support and transportation, but there was no way of finding out until someone helped me. Even Dad was frustrated and not a little annoyed with me for being such a poor accountant. Math was one of his strengths. He had actually been employed as an accountant in the U.S. Army in 1918.

The fact is that I have always hated math, and during all my years in college, though I had a bank account, I never recorded my balance and never knew exactly how much money I had. Being downright abstemious, I spent little money and always figured that there was plenty in the bank. After we were married, Rachel was quite horrified to discover how I had handled my finances in the past, and she relieved me of the frustration of keeping accounts.

During our time in California, a good many speaking opportunities opened up for Kemp and me. We traveled to a number of churches in the southern part of the state to give our testimonies and raise the remaining shares required prior to departure. On the way home from a small church south of Los Angeles, our route took us along the Pacific Ocean. It occurred to me that since I had never been baptized, it would be the prudent and biblical thing to do before going to Asia, where the Japanese, Korean, and Chinese are never considered truly Christians until they have received this sacrament. Since I would presumably be urging the Chinese in Formosa to receive Christ and be baptized, it might be a good idea if I myself were baptized.

We arranged with Dad to hold a baptismal ceremony at a coastal site on the Pacific Ocean. A small company of us drove to the sandy stretches of Venice Beach one Sunday evening. There were four candidates: Kemp, sister Vangie, dear friend Ruth Jeffries, and me. When we arrived at the beach, the moon was only a narrow crescent over the horizon. The tide had brought the surf well up the sandy slopes. We could hear the ominous thunder of the breakers, spewing sand and briny water against the shore.

Immediately, it became obvious that this would be something more than another ordinary baptismal service. A proper, somber, and devotional atmosphere was hindered by the fact that around us on the beach were strewn amorous couples, blanketed together. Notwithstanding these distractions, Dad had a beautiful way of making the Spirit of God at home even when surrounded by unbelievers.

We gathered in a small circle, prayed, and reviewed the significance of the holy rite. We found a small cove-like spot which we thought was sheltered from the violence of the waves. We waded out into the water, which was one moment knee deep but the next moment was engulfing us in the surge of an overwhelming breaker. Kemp was the first to go under, and he came up choking with a mouth full of sand and sea. Vangie was next. A wave caught her and rudely took her under. Ruth presented more of a problem. Not being muscular or athletic by nature, she entered the water with no little fear and trembling. Just as she arose from the initial immersion, a splendid wave took her under for a second blessing. I was the last one to enjoy the unique ceremony. We returned to the dressing rooms well doused, salty and sandy, but knowing for certain that our baptism had been, without doubt, full and sufficient.

Kemp had never been to California, and now as I escorted him about the city to view the famous sights, I was keenly aware of how this glitzy, gaudy, western state differed from the conservative eastern and southern states in which I had lived for most of the last four years. The Golden State has no bondage to tradition. I thought of the legendary Odysseus who journeyed to the magic isle inhabited by lotus eaters. At first he sought to rid himself of their seduction, but the longer he remained the more he was enticed to eat their food and adopt their ways.

We also shopped for crusade necessities, particularly an army surplus sleeping bag and an air mattress. These for the next two years would soften my slumber on floors in the halls and rented rooms where we would hold crusade meetings.

Now it was time to think about the chore of packing, which is part of the warp and woof of missionary life. In our missionary career now spanning over fifty years, we have moved house more than twenty-five times and packed countless suitcases, crates, barrels, and other assorted containers. Packing for a single missionary for a brief term of two years should have been a relatively simple matter. But the task was complicated by the fact that field missionaries regularly asked newcomers and returning colleagues to bring with them all manner of commodities which they could not obtain locally.

In this, my first solo voyage, my luggage would include, along with many the many items requested by missionaries in Asia, a kitchen sink. In my letter to Rachel I wrote:

> *Another milestone is now behind us – packing. After days of buying, banding, crating, marking, weighing, and evaluating, we finally got our stuff safely delivered to the L.A. harbor. I ended up with something over four hundred pounds. Three hundred pounds is supposed to be the maximum load per passenger. Compared to Kemp, however, I had it easy. He was encumbered with a far greater assortment of packages, most of it for missionaries in Japan. His total came to about eight hundred pounds!*

I then followed with this paragraph, which so well reflects the idealism of the novice missionary not yet fully acquainted with the realities of life in a foreign county. Cynically, I wrote:

> *The day of sacrifice on the mission field is all but gone. When the present-day missionary finds himself bereft of his customary cake of Sweetheart soap or box of Rinso or grated coconut, he simply wires the home office and has the goods delivered by the next out-coming candidate. Ah, I remember the old days, days of suffering and sacrifice when the missionary had only the meanest of accommodations. He was housed in a large, untenable, cave-like building without benefit of plumbing, electricity, or even indoor cooking facilities. All clothes he wore*

were fashioned of cheap Indian cotton sewn by a local tailor. Shoes were likewise cobbled by local craftsmen and lacked the luxury of innersoles and cushioned arch support. But all that is gone forever.

Then with some exaggeration I added, "The missionary has traded his Bible for a four-hundred-dollar camera with a hand-ground lens. It seems that the cross of sacrifice has been exchanged for a charge account with Montgomery Ward."

Right: The Asbury Trio, 1929: Byron Crouse, Virgil Kirkpatrick, Eugene Erny

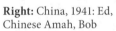

Left: Peking, China, 1937: Eugene, Bob, Esther, Ed

Right: China, 1941: Ed, Chinese Amah, Bob

Left: India days: Esther, Bob, Eugene, Vangie, Ed

Left: India 1943: Esther, Vangie

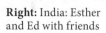

Right: India: Esther and Ed with friends

Right: In Allahabad, India, 2005: Bob, Vangie, Ed

Right: In Allahabad, India, 1992: Ed preaching with interpreter

Right: Los Angeles, California, 1952: Culter Academy basketball team, Ed (back R)

Right: Culter reunion, California, 2003: With a few classmates.

Right: Yosemite Days

Left: Yosemite Park, California, 2007: Half Dome in background

Left: Asbury College, 1956: Ed, pole vaulting

Right: Asbury College, 1957: On campus

Left: Asbury Days

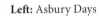

CHAPTER 15

THE VOYAGE

We had booked passage to Japan and Formosa on a Danish freighter, the SS *Laura Maersk*. Our scheduled date of departure was Saturday, August 21. We found the ship docked at a berth in the Los Angeles harbor of San Pedro.

It is customary for all departing missionaries to be accorded a formal farewell at OMS headquarters. Ours was scheduled for Friday afternoon. At coffee time, they had an appropriate ceremony for Kemp and me. Aunt Annie Kartozian, a veteran missionary to China and Taiwan, gave a short speech about adapting to the country and presented each of us with a lovely blanket. The proper name for this very serviceable item is a steamer rug. Mine was a beautiful blue and red plaid, and it continues to serve us many years later.

Before sailing, I had told Rachel I'd call her long-distance from California. This was an extravagance I could ill afford. In our twenty years of missionary service in Taiwan, I don't think we called back to the U.S. more than five or six times. Those were days when long-distance calls were, for missionaries at least, quite prohibitive.

When we arrived at the dock for our departure that Sunday afternoon, a group had already gathered to bid us farewell. A good number from the office had turned out for the occasion and we felt honored. Vangie was crying, and Mom's eyes were full of misty pride. Dad felt proud of me too, I think. They drove away, waving at me until the corner of a warehouse blocked us from their sight. Kemp and I were alone, and Asia was before us. I looked into the soft harbor lights with a rising moon over the mast.

We were up at six the next morning as the ship glided out of the bay. The atmosphere was heavy with mist and no promise of sun. It did not take long for Los Angeles to disappear from our view, and soon the hometown was just an outline and then a small irregularity on the landscape. By the middle of the morning, we were completely surrounded by a universe of water. One forgets about the singular briny wasteland encompassing fully one-third of our world, the endless, unfathomable pool of the Pacific. This little ship was to be our constant companion and home for the next three weeks. We were told that we would not so much as pass an island or see another vessel until we reached Hawaii.

Since high school days, I had taken to writing poetry and acquired a small collection of poems. It has been observed that in most human beings the muses are most active in youth. Later, as people marry and age, these poetic impulses decline and often cease. In English literature, the sea is often synonymous with adventure and romance. On this unforgettable journey, I felt quite often the need to express myself in poetry. There is much time to think about water, a mysteriously wonderful substance possessing an endless repertoire of moods and forever changing its countenance. This inspired the following:

> *God, I love Thy vagrant sea*
>   *What skills Thy hand has taught her*
> *This miracle of endless wave*
>   *This boundless world of water.*

I love this couch upon her breast
   It swells with sweet emotion
A woman's spirit lies ensnared
   Imprisoned in this ocean.

Today she sulks in gloomy gray
   And pulls the clouds above her
Tomorrow night, a water sprite,
   She thrills me like a lover.

But watch her when she softly broods
   Or whimpers like a child
Her temper worse than Satan's curse
   And fully twice as wild.

Our voyage to Asia was now shadowed by news coming over the ship's shortwave on a daily basis. There had been dogfights for months on alternating days over the China Straits. Communist planes were engaging fighter pilots of Chiang Kai-shek's Republic of China. Enemy guns also lobbed shells intended for the offshore islands of Kinmen and Matsu, still in Nationalist hands. All of this had been fairly routine and provoked no particular alarm, a mere formality, simply the Communists' token of their claim to all of China including Formosa and the surrounding islands. Now, however, it was reported that a vast army was massing on the coast, obviously for an invasion. This was no mere military exercise. Knowledgeable observers said that Mao Tse-tung was determined to invade Formosa. Our one consolation lay in the fact that the powerful United States Seventh Fleet was patrolling the straits between the two Chinas.

   As a boy, I had sailed on vessels to Asia. There is a glory about a ship. One who has loved a sturdy vessel and developed an affection for the sea understands Masefield's famous words: "I must go down to the seas again." The salty rail felt familiar against my fingers.

The SS *Laura Maersk* was a fine ship, not a large vessel, only 190 feet from helm to stern and 51 feet wide. She had mastered the sea for over 20 years and glided over the choppy waves like a seasoned sailor, gaining a reputation as a "good riding ship." There was none of the grimy, slovenly quality about her, characteristic of so many freighters. She was manned by a crew of 43 immaculate Danes, rather handsome fellows with a whimsical quality all their own.

The captain was Mr. Schmidt, a broad little chap with a red nose, a twinkle in his eyes, and a sort of dry wit. It is the custom on freighters for chief officers to fraternize with the passengers and have meals together in the small dining room. Chief Officer Hulm sat at our table. He was a quiet man of about forty with a rich vein of good humor in him under his rough exterior. Amazingly well read, he spoke excellent English. I found him the most interesting of the officers. Mr. Nelson, the chief engineer, was a handsome fellow. He had a happy-go-lucky demeanor and was not overly concerned with his obligations and duties. His main objective in life seemed to be to have a good time and take it easy. We asked him rather dutifully if he liked the sea. He looked at us thoughtfully and finally replied, "No." The chief steward was seldom around, and the great mystery, never solved, was what his duties involved. The two cabin boys, Nelson and Peterson, were at our beck and call night and day. All in all, we had a remarkably congenial crew, apparently without a single ill-natured officer in the lot. Everyone maintained an air of courtesy in an effort to keep the very temperamental Yankees in good humor.

Now we come to the passengers. First, there was Dr. Mahlar and his wife. She taught Asian arts at Colombia University, and he – well, no one was quite certain what the good doctor did. He spoke with a British accent and possessed a subtle humor. He spent a good deal of the time boozing it up. Mr. and Mrs.

Erich were middle-aged folk whose calling seemed to be to travel the world on leisurely voyages from one port to another. At present, they were on a four-month tour of Asia and Europe. A single lady, Miss Martin, was a nursing instructor bound for Colombo, Ceylon. She was the only smoker in our group and spent much time carrying on sophisticated conversations, especially with the professor of Asian arts. Then there was Louise Crawford, an accomplished spinster who had taught at Kodaikanal International School, a mission school in India. She acquired an MA in journalism and was on her way to Formosa to teach at Tunghai, a nominally Christian university. A young missionary couple, the Waddingtons, completed the passenger list. They were American Baptists and very compatible with us. We started a Bible study with them and looked forward to times of fellowship.

In my journal, I recorded an impressive and unrealistic daily regimen I set for myself:

1. Read every book you have brought with you, about fifteen.
2. Spend a good share of your time in prayer and soul searching.
3. Continue journaling faithfully and any other writing you feel impressed to do.
4. Write at least one poem a day.
5. Study the Word with renewed zeal, especially the books of John and Acts.
6. Write Rachel every other day.
7. Witness to your fellow passengers and crew at every opportunity.
8. Prepare yourself spiritually for the ministry God

has given and "practice the presence of God" continually. Be prepared to do anything and everything He instructs you to do.

I still remember most of those books that I pored over on that voyage. One was the biography of the great prayer warrior, *Rees Howells: Intercessor* by Norman Grubb. In the Bible college in which he taught in Swansea, Wales, he organized special student prayer teams to wait on God during the great crises of World War II.

Many believed that four turning points during that war were tremendously affected by the prayers of Rees Howells and his students, as well as God's people all over the world. The Holy Spirit, it seemed, had prompted Howells to ask specifically for four things: (l) that Hitler should not invade England (a prayer that was wonderfully fulfilled in the miracle at Dunkirk); (2) that Stalingrad should not be taken (the city never fell despite a myriad of predictions to the contrary); (3) that Moscow would not be taken; and (4) that Alexandria should not be taken. Amazingly, in these four crises, Howells' prayers prevailed. In fact, all these battles proved to be decisive and together formed the turning points of the war.

I also read the biography of David Livingstone, perhaps the most famous of all missionaries. His life and testimony so impacted the British Empire and the world that the entire "dark" continent was opened to the gospel.

While in China, my parents had personally met Jonathan and Rosalind Goforth and were great admirers of that intrepid and devout couple. Aboard ship, I read Jonathan Goforth's biography and then a powerful account of the great revivals in north China entitled *By My Spirit*. Another moving book was a small blue volume, *Giants of the Missionary Trail* by Eugene Harrison. As I read these short biographies, I was deeply impressed with the incomparable thrill of being a partaker in God's calling to be a missionary.

I felt that the Holy Spirit directed me in this choice of reading matter. The messages gave me a deeper hunger than I had ever known to be all that God wanted me to be. At the same time, I confess that reading these books also created in me a convicting sense of inadequacy. The measure of dedication that these men knew was quite beyond my experience. Sometimes I was gripped by a strong sense of condemnation. After searching myself for days, I asked, "What is it that God is trying to say?"

I suppose that in the light of these giants' accomplishments, my calling seemed insignificant. I was convicted too that I lacked boldness. I could not free myself from feelings of inferiority and fears that often turned my lips to clay and frustrated many of my spiritual aspirations. I was greatly encouraged to meditate on the manner in which God enabled Jonathan Goforth to overcome his natural language ineptitude. Could He do the same for me?

I was tremendously stirred as I read of the cost of spiritual power in the lives of great missionaries. The Goforths of China buried five of their infant children in Chinese soil, lost their home half a dozen times, and suffered incredible hardships. The same with William Carey, Adoniram Judson, Henry Martyn, John Hyde, and James Chalmers. Wherever men and women have dared to yield to God's highest for their lives, it has cost them a heavy price.

Now the thing I was struggling with was still a question of whether I cared enough for this power to pay the price. I thought I paid a price in leaving my sweetheart for two years, but the Spirit was beginning to show me that this preliminary sacrifice could be a steppingstone to much greater things for His sake.

I was challenged to think of the cost of obedience for Henry Martyn. He left his beloved in England because her mother refused to allow her to accompany him to India. He died at the age of thirty-two without the comfort of a companion or the joy of ever seeing even a meager harvest. Chalmers was bludgeoned to death by cannibals in New Guinea and promptly eaten. John Hyde spent most of his life in India on his knees, often praying nine hours a day. Now a question plagued me: Did I want the anointing of God enough to pay the price, which included an unrelenting and tireless prayer life, hours on my knees to the neglect of family and friends and that which is cherished?

Did I want God's blessing and power that badly? After all, there are thousands of "good missionaries" doing an acceptable job without all of these heroics. Not everyone is called to be a spiritual giant. These were days of preparation and soul searching for me.

On this voyage, I learned many interesting facts about the ocean from my friend Mr. Hulm, the chief officer. A nautical mile is six thousand feet, and the ocean beneath us is about three miles deep. Its deepest point is off the Hawaiian Islands, and there it measures six miles straight down. Our boat travelled at about seventeen knots per hour, which was twenty miles per hour, and the international dateline is not, as some believe, a visible marker in the water.

Sunsets on the Pacific are a lavish display that is almost impossible to put into words, but one evening I tried with this poem.

> I saw God put the sun to bed
>   Upon a couch of gold and red.
> He beckoned to the eager night
>   And softly dimmed the royal light.
>
> A crimson tide swept higher, higher
>   In fields of iridescent fire
> And gleaming fingers clean and proud
>   Embrace the coral reefs of cloud.

THE VOYAGE

> *Then comet, frenzied envoys flew*
>   *Along a dome of crystal blue*
>   *Across the circle of the west*
>   *They fell together in a crest.*
>
> *So in the face of velvet night*
>   *I marked the battlefield of light*
> *A war of intermingled hue*
>   *With legions gold and crimson, blue.*
>
> *The jealous ocean leaped to hold*
>   *The wasted pools of liquid gold*
> *And out across the briny caves*
>   *She flung the light from wave to wave.*

For several days, I labored over a small volume designed to improve one's vocabulary. I learned that we have two vocabularies: (1) words that we know and recognize, and (2) words which are incorporated into our writing and speaking, called the active vocabulary. The first vocabulary is usually three times as large as the active one. I find this kind of study fascinating and resolved to consciously seek to broaden my vocabulary, both that of word recognition and words that are actively employed.

By the first week in September, we were nearing the coast of Japan. We had been on the ship for more than two weeks. All of my life I have regarded this first voyage to Formosa as a most useful and precious interlude, prior to setting foot as a missionary on foreign soil. It was wonderful to have those weeks completely unfettered and far removed from the accouterments of rutted living. I had been sort of deposited on a temporary plateau of exhilaration, even ecstasy, which I realize now is passing and cannot endure.

Chapter 16

JAPAN

As we neared Japan, where a portion of our passengers would be disembarking, Kemp and I were made aware of the fact that among some of our shipmates there was a great deal of extra-curricular activity going on. The good captain was demonstrating his great fondness for drink and little concern for morality. His partner in these festivities was Miss Martin, the middle-aged nurse heading for Ceylon. This disturbed us in that the captain was a married man with a family of which he boasted.

God gave many opportunities to witness to the Danish crew, as well as to fellow passengers. As I prepared my message for the Sunday morning service, the Devil told me that I had been misled in the choice of my text inasmuch as most of our fellow passengers would likely not be present to hear the message. On the previous Sunday, only the faithful, religiously minded ones had been there to worship.

Since I felt I had nothing else to preach, however, I prepared diligently, writing out the entire sermon in manuscript form as had become my habit. That morning Kemp led the singing and under sweet inspiration sang "Ship Ahoy." God's Spirit was faithful in spite of my trembling faith. Not only were the good doctor and his wife in attendance but incredibly, so was Miss Martin, looking a bit sheepish. Later the chief steward also joined us. The words came boldly as though assisted by a blessed "Presence." I believed that needy hearts were moved and Christians in our company were stirred afresh.

These thoughts inspired the following verse from my pen:

> *Oh, holy God, we plead Thy word*
>   *Thou wield the flaming two-edged sword*
> *The building of the soul be rent*
>   *Undo the sluggish heart's intent.*
>
> *The sacred sword in Calvary bathed*
>   *Shall not return to Thee unscathed*
> *Smite now the idols long endeared*
>   *Unstop the unused fount of tears.*
>
> *Now purge my being, set it free*
>   *And give me of Thy liberty.*

On September 6, the SS *Laura Maersk* docked at Yokohama, the port of Tokyo. After two weeks of shoreless seas, the sight of land was welcomed indeed, as we watched the great island empire emerge from the mist, shadowy at first but gaining definition. The rough temper of the ocean subsided and we found ourselves bosomed in the bay. It was so still, almost turning glassy. Little crafts seemed to emerge from nowhere, small fishing vessels and then larger crafts, odd-looking barges, big-funneled inland freighters. Soon the narrow waterway became crowded. Across the mouth of the breakwater, two large tankers prostrated themselves.

Then came the typical sounds and clutter of the Asia where I had lived and grown up. This gave me that old familiar feeling, something akin to the sensation of returning home after a long absence. We watched from the topmost deck, a small crowd of us all registering different emotions and responses to the scene. It was twilight, and the first flickers of harbor lights appeared in the oil that floated upon the waters.

The blinking eyes of the great city opened to us. The boats and harbor vessels chugged busily about us, and nostalgic guttural utterances of the coolies broke the still night air. It was Japan, much as I had remembered it but greatly changed, as I was to learn. We anchored in the middle of the harbor where a barge-like vessel would convey baggage and freight to the shore.

Once our ship had anchored, a launch pulled up alongside us. Soon enough Helmut Schultz appeared around the corner of the deck and started bellowing, "Asbury College, this is the school we love!" Then we caught sight of Ernie Kilbourne, followed by Lester Ike and his son. We had a real reception committee. After the usual disembarking procedures, we managed to get away, transported by the launch to shore and then through the traffic-knotted streets. We wended our way through the prolific and ever-congested alleyways. Ernie, who had grown up in Asia and was an old hand at "taxi" maneuvers, chauffeured us along at an alarming rate back to the broader boulevards with familiar stoplights, and then into the meandering streets with quaint shops and dark corners where our headlights only slightly embarrassed groups of men casually urinating in the gutters.

This was Japan, a most curious blend of Eastern and Western ways. It seemed strange, for instance, to see a modern telephone booth positioned under sprawling pagoda-like structures centuries old. Here again I encountered the Asian charm that I always associate with my boyhood in China and India.

In Tokyo, I stayed with Helmut and Norma Jean for about a week while our ship made additional stops at various ports in Japan. That let me enjoy a leisurely visit and gave me sufficient time to see a few of the notable sights, but not Mount Fuji – too much mist. The weather was hot and sticky, although it was nothing compared to Alabama in the summertime.

Ernie and Vi Kilbourne took me shopping. First, we visited a curio store and appraised a great display of trinkets, lamps, bowls, dishes, brass, and a million and one other things of interest, all priced incredibly low. I wished I had a hundred dollars to spend. We then went for lunch in an exotic hotel and from there to another shopping center with paintings. The lovely Japanese watercolors truly excited my admiration, as did exquisite pearl jewelry along with jade and lacquerware.

From there we drove to one of Tokyo's air-conditioned department stores with all the features of the finest shops in the world. The Japanese are marvelous craftsmen, and everywhere, we saw an impressive display of modern electronic devices: radios, TVs, phonographs, and Nikon cameras. Art supplies always capture my interest, and I purchased a set of watercolors. The basement of the store was a food bazaar. There we found everything from typical U.S. snacks and sandwiches to characteristically Japanese seafood, including squid and octopus that was pickled, roasted, basted, steamed, and stuffed.

Tokyo was a modern miracle city rising from the ashes of World War II. It had now gained the distinction of being the largest city in the world with a population of about ten million. They were endeavoring to make everything the biggest, best, and most impressive: hotels, stores, factories, train systems, and now a large TV antenna shaped something like the Eiffel Tower.

Still there were anomalies. In the shadow of the giant department stores were the vestiges of heathenism and bawdy districts of licensed prostitution, small squalid huts, and people still carrying on primitive handicraft-making of mat and basket weaving. And everywhere was evidence that this was still the dominion of Satan and not an easy place for missionaries. Temptations to luxury and ease were just as much a factor in Tokyo as in Los Angeles. The pace of life was typical of the great cities of the world. It was hard to find time to pray, and the threats of materialism and secularism were evident everywhere.

That evening, however, I did have a profitable time of prayer with Helmut. "I am so thankful for a man of his caliber," I wrote in my journal, "one who always places the emphasis on living in the Spirit and demonstrating the power of God. I am now eager to begin my Taiwan ministry. I am excited but also fearful, feeling more than ever unqualified for the demands."

While in Japan, Helmut suggested that it would be a worthwhile experience for me to visit one of the Every Creature Crusade teams in the area. That Sunday we took the train to Nagoya where an ECC campaign was being conducted by Kelly Toth and his team.

Like Tokyo traffic, Japanese trains are memorable. We found ourselves in a third-class compartment sitting across from a grandmother whose wrinkles attested to a very long life. She was an amiable sort with a mouth full of gold and a charming wrinkled visage. She had no knowledge of English, but through our friend Saki-san, the Ikes' maid, we were informed that she had a son in California. This proved a quaint and charming encounter. She promptly opened her lunch, shared her cookies with us, and offered us cigarettes.

Soon we were at Nagoya. The taxi hurried us through the busy thoroughfares to a remote section of town. The OMS church was partially obscured by a huddle of typical Japanese dwellings. The service was about to begin as we entered. Diminutive desks and benches served as pews. We all squeezed our knees together, contracted our bodies, and positioned ourselves for the service. It was conducted completely in Japanese and although I understood nothing other than the text, I could nevertheless sense the presence of the Spirit and agreed with Helmut who said he would rather worship under these conditions with God's presence than in the most beautiful of our cathedrals in the U.S.

After introductions and incessant bowing and smiling, we gathered around the foot-high table for Sunday dinner. The main course was much to my liking, but the introduction of bean cakes and tofu soup was almost too much even for my very adaptable stomach. The insipid artificial sweetness of the cakes and the foul smell of the sour bean curd soup wreaked havoc with my appetite. I began to think deeply about the challenges ahead of me – a full two years of this kind of food!

Preparation for the evening service entailed a circular jaunt around town with members of the team beating a drum, playing an accordion, and passing out tracts. One of the team members carried a portable loud speaker and announced the service.

There were about thirty in the tent that night. I was asked to give a word of testimony. I felt keenly the futility of my words. The language barrier can be a terribly frustrating thing. Helmut gave a warm and heartfelt message, followed by an impassioned appeal from his interpreter. The train schedule required we leave before the conclusion of the service, so we headed back to the more-crowded-than-ever train. All of us but the ladies were obliged to stand on the way home.

Some mountaineers, after a weekend trek, were sprawled across the aisle and under the seats in a most disconcerting fashion. This made the passage from one end of the car to the other a near impossibility. We arrived home very tired and ready to sack out in good old American style.

The following week, Les Ike shepherded me to the central train station where I embarked for the southern metropolis of Osaka. Here I changed trains and in a few minutes found myself in the sister city of Kobe. This should have marked the conclusion of my Japan travels, but it turned out to be the most grievous part of my day's journey.

To ascertain the location of my ship, I called the *Maersk* office to enquire the whereabouts of the SS *Laura Maersk*.

There followed some alarming information. The ship, I was informed, was not at Kobe, as per the original schedule, but rather at Dock 4 in Osaka, or possibly not at the dock at all but rather anchored out in the harbor due to an approaching typhoon. Remembering the brevity of the ride between Osaka and Kobe by train, I decided to spend a few yen and risk a taxi ride to the pier. Alas, fifteen hundred yen later, I found myself at the far end of the city of Osaka, a one-and-a-half-hour taxi ride from Kobe.

But this was not the end of my travails. The dock man knew very little English but finally managed to explain that my ship had left the harbor at 2:00 p.m. the previous day. He assured me that now it would be docked in Kobe. The taxi now commenced a long and tedious ride back through the densely populated city.

It was seven o'clock when I arrived at the dock. What appeared to be my ship, however, was a sister ship, the *Ellen*. Finally, down toward the extremity of the pier, I discerned the outline of another vessel dimly blue in the misty illumination of the harbor. I picked out the white inscription on the bow. With great relief, I read the words "SS *Laura Maersk*." I paid the taxi man my last yen, which was insufficient to cover the sum that appeared on his meter. He was not too happy about this but soon understood that I absolutely and truly had no more money on my person, not a single yen. And neither was I permitted to board the ship to get more money and then return to the pier to pay him the full amount.

I made my way up the old familiar gangplank and soon encountered my fellow passengers. They met me with many exciting tales of the beauties and quaintness of Japan. It almost felt like a family reunion.

A typhoon was indeed heading our way. The captain was eager to be out of Kobe harbor for safety's sake. We weighed anchor at 8:00 p.m. and slipped out into the dark waters of the

Pacific. The sight of the great sea and the lights shimmering along the shore will always remain with me. The view inspired the following poem which I titled "Leaving Kobe":

> She wears a million-lighted gown
> > To bid us sayonara
> Composed of bucketfuls of stars
> > Flung out along her feet.
>
> Becoming silver swords and pools of gold
> > Upon the harbor's breast
> A bolder, brilliant ruby broach
> > Winks out a last farewell.
>
> Above us, the new beginnings
> > Of a moon
> A good omen the sailors say.
>
> The last night's storm has
> > Tantrummed up the coast
> Leaving to us a welcome briny boulevard.
>
> The shore becomes a luminous mist
> > Fast fading now
> And once again upon my ear
> > The sea-time songs of coursing wind
> And palavering wave upon the bow.
>
> Good-bye sweet land
> > We part thy winsome company
> The busy little tug and barge
> > Must look for other friends.

The ship set its bow south towards the island of Formosa. For me, the excitement of approaching my destination made it more and more difficult to accomplish much in the way of reading and writing. Psalm 46, Livingstone's favorite, became very meaningful: *The heathen raged, the kingdoms were moved: he uttered his voice, the earth melted* (KJV). Also Psalm 91: *For he shall give his angels charge over thee, to keep thee in all thy ways. They shall bear thee up in their hands, lest thou dash thy foot against a stone* (KJV).

I attempted to write a play, something I had done during my college days. This featured the life of America's first foreign missionary, Adoniram Judson. Years later when I read my creation, I blushed at the purple prose and felt grateful that it had never been published.

Chapter 17

FORMOSA WELCOME

A day out of Keelung Harbor, I almost hated to see my time aboard ship come to a close, but I knew I would grow impatient if the voyage were further prolonged. Those were grand days. With the voyage ending, a new chapter was about to begin.

Is this the kind of work for which I'm cut out? I wondered. It was mostly public work and I was definitely not a "public man." I have the heart, I think, of an old-fashioned recluse. Yet I was positive that this was the place where I should be.

The ship was delayed in docking. Formosa emerged at last, a gray, elongated, jagged hump on the horizon, shrouded with white mist. We had a final Sunday morning service. I had not had time to properly prepare so I used a favorite text, the same I had chosen on a street corner in Frankfort, Kentucky: *For the preaching of the cross is to them that perish foolishness; but unto us which are saved it is the power of God.*

Before long, a crew member bounded up the companionway, calling my name. I was summoned to the side, and there bobbing below in a sampan I spied Rollie Rice, exuberant as always, waving excitedly. With him were Uncle Meredith Helsby and Aunt Christine. They had been in Taiwan since 1956. I waved a greeting and had to pinch myself that I was at journey's end at last.

In time, my greeters came aboard and helped me to locate sundry items which I had inadvertently neglected to pack. Aunt Christine toted my football and, with others carrying hand luggage, I bade farewell to the SS *Laura Maersk*.

The Grand Hotel was our first stop, and there I was feted a lavish welcome dinner in the elaborate dining room. This hotel, impressive even then, has since been reconstructed and today is regarded as one of the most beautiful and luxurious hotels in the world. It was built primarily for the use of important international guests of the Nationalist Party and was under the direction of Madame Chiang Kai-shek.

After a sumptuous dinner featuring favorite Chinese dishes, we took taxis to the train station where we boarded the 8:20 p.m. southbound express for Taichung where the OMS work was situated. When the coaches finally pulled in, we found our reserve seats amidst the usual melee of baggage and people and were soon cruising along at considerable speed past the honeycomb-like refugee shacks that bordered the railroad line. The train reminded me of Japan. There was the same impressive service with hot tea and hot washcloths to keep weary travelers clean and content.

Now, with the wonderful voyage behind me and my first Every Creature Crusade yet to be launched, I found myself in what was, apart from the rigors of language study, a delightful four-month interim.

This proved a time for orientation to life in Formosa as well as to the OMS campus. I was soon made to feel quite at home among the congenial missionary family, most of whom were "old-China hands," foreigners who had previously resided on the China mainland. In the late 1930s, many had been my parents' colleagues. We had enjoyed their companionship when they passed through OMS headquarters in Los Angeles.

The city of Taichung was halfway down the island. The

nine-acre campus on which the Central Taiwan Theological College was located was strikingly lovely. The property had formerly been owned by the Japanese, but after World War II, it reverted to China. Bud and Hazel Kilbourne had pioneered the OMS work in Taiwan. Their son, Elmer, thanks to his family's friendship with the mayor of the city, managed to purchase the land for an incredibly low price.

When I arrived, the former farmland had been transformed into a lush green oasis of lawn with school buildings and homes located around the perimeter of the property and shaded by poinsettia trees. Behind the missionary homes was a small swimming pool where, during the hot, non-air-conditioned summer months, missionaries enjoyed respite and recreation.

In time, OMS's Taichung campus became a mecca for travelers and attracted many noted religious and missionary leaders. Among them were Bob Pierce of World Vision, the Billy Graham evangelistic team, and noted athletes such as members of the Venture for Victory basketball teams.

But of all the visitors, the one who most impacted my life was a plain, stocky, and then-relatively unknown Dutch woman, a former POW in a Nazi extermination camp. I had never heard the name Corrie ten Boom before that October afternoon when I attended a home meeting at which she was speaking.

After tea, this plain, unassuming lady with a thick Dutch accent, gray hair pulled back in a bun, and a sparkle in her eyes positioned herself on a chair with a big Bible spread atop her knees. From her first words, I felt a gripping intensity in her simple expressions that reflected an unusual intimacy wrung from the incredible suffering and tortuous circumstances that had so wedded her to Jesus. Her message was just what I needed. She recounted some of her death camp experiences, telling how God used her to win even her cruel guards to Christ. Only 20 percent of the prisoners survived. During the war, she had lost her father, sister, brother, and nephew. But she came through it all "not somehow but triumphantly."

A short time later, she became famous, due in part to her book and film, *The Hiding Place*. She was used throughout the world in a marvelous ministry, particularly among missionaries and Christian workers. Her victory amidst terrible testing convicted me for my frequent complaints and small trials. She emphasized the fact that "discouragement is sin." Other quotes I jotted down were: "Keep looking up and kneeling down"; "In the valley of the shadow there must be a light or there would be no shadow"; "We don't know what's coming but we do know who's coming"; and "I don't have a great faith, just a small faith in a great God."

The next Sunday, Corrie spoke in the Taichung English service, which a good number of missionaries attended. She quoted Charles Spurgeon who said, "Oh, to have one soul under heavenly cultivation, no wilderness but a garden of God walled around by grace, planted by instruction, visited by love, weeded by heavenly discipline, and guarded by divine power. One soul thus favored is prepared to yield fruit unto the glory of God."

She closed her message with an anonymous poem that I had not heard before. Including it in her book made it a favorite among Christians everywhere.

> *My life is but a weaving*
>   *Between my God and me.*
> *I do not choose the colors*
>   *He worketh steadily.*
>
> *Oft-times He weaveth sorrow*
>   *And I in foolish pride*
> *Forget He sees the upper*
>   *And I the underside.*

Not till the loom is silent
　And the shuttles cease to fly
Will God unroll the canvas
　And explain the reason why.

The dark threads are as needful
　In the skillful weaver's hand
As the threads of gold and silver
　In the pattern He has planned.

I was housed with the Helsbys, reminiscent of my first days at Asbury. Uncle Med and I had many things in common, including photography and tennis. He and Aunt Christine, with their small daughter Sandra, had been imprisoned by the Japanese during World War II in the famous Weihsien internment camp where their neighbor and friend was the famous Olympian Eric Liddell (of *Chariots of Fire* fame). Being in their home these months was delightful.

Sandra, their oldest daughter, had just graduated from Morrison Academy and was a freshman at Roberts Wesleyan College. Gary was in junior high; Sheryl was in elementary school; and the youngest, Gordie, was a frisky three-year-old who attended a Chinese kindergarten.

I soon discovered what everyone on the compound already knew – that Gordie was a genius at mischief and had acquired a reputation almost equal to that of Dennis the Menace. Every day, he devised sundry pranks and had an inventive agenda. One morning, when the Bible school students were in class, he collected all the keys, along with pens and pencils that he could find in the dormitories, and deposited them in the swimming pool.

Next door to us were Uri and Edna Chandler and their two teenagers, Phil and Carolyn, both students at Morrison Academy. Edna had been a dear friend of Mother's in Peking.

Uri, who had mastered pure Mandarin, had been a member of Dad's early Great Village Campaign in North China.

Next to the Chandlers lived the Rices, veterans of both China and Japan. During the early 1950s, they had lived directly across the street from us at OMS headquarters in Los Angeles. The Rices' house became like a second home to me. Inimitable and unique Mildred became a dear friend and confidant. Their two sons, Ed and David, were students at Morrison Academy, and daughter, Kathy, whom I had dated in Los Angeles, was now a freshman at Asbury College. Rollie, without question one of the most zealous and devout as well as absent-minded people I have ever known, was to be my director in the upcoming crusade.

Added to this number were two single ladies, also veterans of years in China. Both have an honored place in my memory as favorite "aunts." Annie Kartozian, of Armenian parentage, had a special love for missionary kids and knew scores of OMS MKs by name, even remembering their birthdays. Diminutive Arleta Miller, whose stature measured something short of five feet, was among the gentlest and sweetest creatures God ever made. For years, she told me, she had prayed for me regularly by name. She also prayed for the Chinese people who came to Christ through our ministries.

In general, I found the beauty of Formosa exceeded that of Japan. Prior to arrival, I had known very little about this island. In a very short time, through conversation and reading, I began to acquaint myself with the history and geography of the small island (about the size of Maryland) that had for the past half-century been much contested.

Formosa, which today is properly known by its Chinese name of Taiwan, is located in the South China Sea, about 100 miles across the straits from the China mainland. It is believed that the first Europeans to see the island were Portuguese sailors who arrived in 1544. The towering mountainous and forested beauty of the island inspired them to name it Ilha Formosa, which means "beautiful island." *Taiwan*, the Chinese name, means "terraced bay."

When Communists overran the mainland in 1949, Taiwan became the refuge for the Chinese Nationalists, who were "temporarily in exile." Generalissimo Chiang Kai-shek, who escaped with most of his defeated army to the island, made Taipei the capital of his government, the Republic of China, and put the island under martial law. The United States with its Seventh Fleet served as a mighty wall of protection for Chiang's government against the Communists.

Taiwan, as well as Quemoy and Matsu, the smaller offshore islands, cover 13,885 square miles. The main island is 235 miles long and 90 miles wide. It has 555 miles of coastline and thickly forested mountains which cover 80 percent of the island and boast some of the richest timberlands in the world. The mountain ranges run north to south and have about 30 peaks rising over 10,000 feet, the highest of which at 13,113 feet is snow-capped Yushan (known to Westerners as Mount Morrison).

Taiwan's east coast possesses some of the world's steepest coastal cliffs rising several thousand feet straight up from the sea. Short, swift rivers slash gorges down to the Pacific. On the narrow western coast, presently home to most of the twenty-one million Chinese, is a plain about twenty miles wide with soil so fertile that it is compared to the rich San Fernando Valley of California.

Taiwan's climate is subtropical with humid summers from May through September and temperatures usually ranging from eighty to ninety-five degrees. Winters, however, in the largely unheated homes can feel very cold with temperatures occasionally dropping into the fifties or even the forties. During the summer monsoons, we experienced rainfall such as I had never seen. Continuous downpours can inundate the island

and have dumped as much as twenty inches of rain in two days. This actually happened during my time there.

When I first arrived in Taiwan, there were twelve million inhabitants of whom nearly two-thirds were designated Taiwanese. These were Chinese from the Fukien Province who had come to the island in migratory waves dating back to the seventh century. When I arrived in 1958, most of the people spoke a Fukienese dialect known in Taiwan as Taiwanese. Refugees from the China mainland in 1949, about 20 percent of the population, spoke Mandarin, which was then designated the official, approved language for the entire island.

In addition, there were nearly two hundred thousand aborigines. These people of Malo-Polynesian descent are without question the original inhabitants of the island. With the arrival of the more advanced civilization from China, the aborigines were displaced, driven up into the mountain areas, and divested of their land. Hence, they are still called mountain people. Though a primitive civilization and largely illiterate, they have been far more receptive to the gospel than the Chinese. At present, nearly 80 percent of the seven Taiwanese tribes are Christian.

At the time of my arrival, the Taiwanese people and the mainlanders, who had fled to Taiwan to escape the Communists, were sharply divided. In taking over the island in 1948-49, the mainlanders had assumed virtually all political authority and rights. A revolt by the native Taiwanese in 1948 against the mainland domination had been put down with terrible violence resulting in a notorious massacre.

During my first years in Taiwan, there was a great deal of hostility between these two groups of people. In subsequent years, however, as minority mainlanders were of necessity forced to intermarry with the Taiwanese, much of this hostility has dissipated. Now the Taiwanese majority has gained a great deal of voice and power in the government and administration, even electing the nation's presidents.

After the Portuguese arrived in the sixteenth century, the Dutch occupied the island in 1624 and established a large fort in the city of Tainan, the remains of which can still be seen today.

Taiwan's ancient hero is Koxinga, a bi-racial Japanese-Chinese military leader who led an army from China to liberate the island in 1661. Despite the so-called impregnable Dutch fort, Koxinga, with his fleet of junks, arrived suddenly, overthrowing the Dutch and returning Taiwan to Chinese rule. This resulted in a terrible slaughter and the expulsion of all foreigners.

The churches that had been established by the Dutch were destroyed, Christian believers were persecuted, and a number of Dutch priests were actually crucified. The crosses to which the priests were nailed were paraded with much festivity through the towns and cities of Taiwan.

These missionaries, despite their zeal, neglected to translate the Bible into the language of the people. As a result, what had once been a rather substantial Christian church disappeared, leaving hardly a trace of the first missionary effort to Christianize Taiwan.

This marked the end of foreign intrusion until 1895 when Japan, militarily powerful and with its eyes on an empire, arrived to subjugate Taiwan, having already occupied Korea. The rich island was actually the spoils of the Sino-Japanese War of 1895 in which Chinese forces succumbed to the well-armed Japanese military. Japan ruled the island as a colony through World War II.

The work of One Missionary Society in Taiwan dates back to the late 1920s when the island was governed by the Japanese. During this period, the expanding OMS-related church in Japan had sent missionaries to Taiwan, starting a number of churches in major cities. These churches, though primarily for Japanese colonists, also attracted good numbers of Taiwanese. Our early church leaders, both Chinese and tribal, were educated in the OMS-related seminary in Tokyo.

Following World War II and the Communist takeover, many missionaries from China relocated to Taiwan. In Taichung, the Mission and Taiwanese leaders who were trained during the Japanese era worked together to establish the Bible school and sent out evangelistic teams to plant churches. It was within this context that the Every Creature Crusade, of which I was now a part, began working.

CHAPTER 18

FIRST IMPRESSIONS

First impressions, as the saying goes, are lasting, and for me those early days in Taichung were indeed my most impressionable.

Along the street, directly in front of the main gate of the Central Taiwan Bible Training Institute campus flowed an amazing jumble of traffic. Knotted caravans of bicycles meandered in and out of the profuse tangle of three-wheeled bicycle-like conveyances called pedicabs, piled high with not only people but also freight of every description. Pedestrians blithely picked their way through a menagerie of vehicles with unconcern, bolting quickly at the beep of a motorcycle or an occasional automobile.

Bordering the street on either side were curious little stalls for sidewalk trade. Corners of the street and walkways were occupied by proprietors of mobile businesses. An old-looking fellow with a bamboo pole over his shoulders carried a portable restaurant. A bearded, jaundiced man strode by bellowing his advertisement of vegetables and various foodstuffs. All this was accompanied by the roar of motorcycles, the pitter-patter of slippers on the sidewalk, and the clack of wooden sandals.

The more respectable stores were positioned under the balconies that protruded over the sidewalk. Notices of these establishments were posted on signs and billboards cluttering the multitude of pillars and support arches. To me, everything was disconcertingly busy but also congenial. From doorways issued the sound of shop banter, the squall of a baby hanging in a cloth pouch from his mother's back blending with the high-pitched chatter of schoolboys as they contended with traffic, and crowds on their way to and from school.

In narrow alleys I encountered market places with a coagulation of shoppers busily selecting groceries while haggling over prices. This was the Taichung "supermarket," boasting every bit as much color and personality as a Kroger's display. A local fishmonger displayed great hunks of pink tuna looking to me very much like a rich-veined block of mahogany. Large piles of fish with glittering scales were stacked high according to size and species alongside fruit of every imaginable variety.

A grandma sporting a basket-like straw bonnet smiled a toothless grin and selected a handful of greens for her shopping bag. In market areas, traffic hardly seemed to move. It simply merged and emerged. Daily travel necessitated practical skills of negotiating vehicles through the maze of humanity.

Clothing was a curious blend of Western and Asian. Men had turned almost entirely to Western shirts and slacks of indifferent size and cut. Trousers were often too large and far from form fitting. As a result, pants were bunched at the waist and drawn together with a narrow, constricting belt. Women, however, often wore the traditional Chinese chipao or sheath dress, which was high at the neck but featured long slits up the sides.

My first exposure to Taichung temples filled me with dismay. I had forgotten the dark blend of animism and folk religion that constitutes temple worship. It divests the worshiper of precious coins and gives them instead only the silent ache of superstition, fear, and emptiness. All of this would be but a curious display of Asian taste were it not for the hopeful worshipers standing obsequiously and with folded hands before the fearful and hideous wooden divinities.

We watched the worshipers and soon felt a great sorrow. We stood dumb and hurting, and there was nothing one could do but watch, wonder, sigh, and ask again, *Why do the heathen rage and the people imagine a vain thing?*

A small woman clasped a sheaf of burning incense and waved the sticks in halting rhythmic motion. There was earnestness in her face, truly the weight of the centuries on her shoulders. Her step was slow and plodding as she moved toward the foremost idol. Her lips moved. It was something that she had repeated countless times. It came out all tangled with the wisps of incense smoke. A stooped fellow tossed half-moon-shaped disks on the cement floor. He did it once and then again and a third time, noting always the position in which the pieces landed. A shrunken grandmother extracted a long stick from an oblong vase and took it to the priest to read her fortune. This was worship.

The instruments of sound were not being employed. They would be saved for a more significant occasion. The gourd-like drum would be sounded in dull and insistent cries to wake the slothful god from his slumbers. Perhaps the ponderous overhead drum would be sounded or the great drums suspended from the rafters would be vigorously beat until their echoes extended to the remotest part of the neighborhood.

Uncle Meredith and I stepped outside the temple where squat stone dragons guarded the doorways and holy script had been chiseled into the pillars. We saw two furnaces emitting yellow tongues of flame, which danced merrily over the stony surfaces. These furnaces were for the burning of temple money, which was said to somehow furnish currency for dead ancestors, the value of the money supposedly being transmitted by fire and smoke to the spirit world.

These are scenes we cannot afford to become accustomed to.

Although I took very little by way of personal baggage to the field, I made the grievous mistake of shipping a single trunk. This, I discovered, meant going to the port city of Keelung to extract it from customs. This sounds simple but was actually a chore fraught with humiliations and trials.

Uri Chandler kindly agreed to accompany me on this onerous errand. We took the evening train to Taipei. Early the next morning we were on our way to the port city of Keelung. We had employed an agent from the China Travel Service to accompany us. We commenced the daylong pilgrimage from desk to desk in the old, overheated customs house.

As we placed my papers before each official, the man with raised eyebrows very slowly eyed them, mulled over them, and then officiously proceeded to affix his "chop" (seal) on the documents. These papers would then require the same treatment by the next official. Some of these men reviewed the papers with a critical eye, asking pertinent questions regarding the goods' value and age before passing them to the man at the adjacent desk. Soon the morning was gone, and everyone disappeared for a long lunch break and brief siesta. Then the wearisome task was resumed.

Altogether, I counted more than thirty desks in that customs house, before which most required our presence. We later learned that with millions of retired servicemen in Taiwan, the government felt obliged to offer them some kind of employment. To accomplish this, they created a tangle of bureaucracy that defied imagination. If even one disgruntled official in an uncooperative mood found fault with my documents, the whole process would be delayed. Some foreigners described this ordeal as the "belly crawl."

In the middle of the afternoon, we finally secured my trunk and saw it safely loaded on the train for Taichung. The only items on which I was charged duty were car tires for an OMS vehicle and coffee for Mildred Rice.

From Keelung we boarded the 3:10 p.m. train for Taipei. This was no express train but rather a local one that stopped at every junction. As the carriages filled, our bodies were constricted, and I was pressed against a hardback bench with my knees intertwined with the Chinese gentleman on the opposite bench. Traveling like this was very wearing, reminding me of boyhood travels on the famous East India Railroad in India. To help recover from the ordeal of the day, Uri hailed a taxi, and we headed to the Grand Hotel for a sumptuous Chinese meal. Late that night we finally arrived back in Taichung.

The powers that be (which in OMS means the field committee) had already decreed that I was to study Taiwanese. It was an unusual mandate at a time when most missionaries on the island studied Mandarin. This was understandable, however, since my assignment was to work and live almost exclusively with Taiwanese-speaking people. The churches we planted would be Taiwanese – pastors, members, and the language of worship – all Taiwanese.

Nobody warned me of the Herculean path on which I was about to embark. While Mandarin is a less complicated and mellifluous tongue, Taiwanese was closest, I was told, to ancient Chinese, full of unpronounceable rasping and nasal sounds, aspirates, and glottal stops. Worst of all, whereas Mandarin has four simple tones, tones that seldom change, Taiwanese has eight tones, all of which must constantly change. By this I mean one character alone is one tone, but when that same character is combined with another character it can change to an altogether different tone.

Many Westerners, in puzzlement, ask why all the different tones. The answer is simple. Many ancient languages have a very limited number of basic sounds. Linguistics experts call

Chinese a "sound-poor" language. To write all the sounds in the Taiwanese dialect requires only sixteen letters of the English alphabet. With so few sounds, how does one go about creating a sufficiently large vocabulary? A single sound is assigned many meanings, depending on the tone in which it is uttered. For instance, while *ma* in the rising third tone means "horse," in the abrupt fifth tone it means "to scold." This can be a tricky business for the foreigner. The words for *buy* and *sell* are identical in sound, but *bey* in the second tone means "to buy," and in a lower tone it means "to sell."

To the new learner of a Chinese dialect, this can result in embarrassing and hilarious anecdotes. Hudson Taylor, after he had recently arrived in China and had begun to study Chinese, asked his servant to buy him a chicken. Late that afternoon the poor man returned with the troubling news that he had searched the entire city and could not find the desired item. In time, Taylor learned that the word for *chicken* and *concubine* are identical in sound but have only slight tonal differences. The cook's quest for a concubine for the foreigner had met with blank stares and angry rejection everywhere.

To this confusion is added the feature of homonyms. In English the words *hair* and *hare* have the same sound but different meanings. Likewise, in Chinese, the same sound and tone may have a variety of meanings as well. I looked up the word *te* in my Taiwanese dictionary and discovered that this one simple sound in the various tones had more than thirty different meanings!

One hundred and fifty years ago, one of the pioneer missionaries to China, the Reverend William Milne, called the study of the Chinese language "a task requiring bodies of iron, lungs of brass, heads of oak, hands of spring steel, eyes of eagles, hearts of apostles, memories of angels, and the lives of Methuselahs."

The ECC schedule allowed me only three months for language

study, and I spent three hours every morning with my language teachers. John Hung was the first. I was told he would probably be my interpreter when the crusade commenced in January. Unfortunately, this never materialized and finding a substitute for John was the subject of great lamentation. John's cousin was my other teacher. Both of these young men were about my age and had remarkably good English.

I fashioned all kinds of study aids. I created vocabulary cards by the score. I tried shreds of conversation with maids and anyone who would put up with me. Sometimes the task was very discouraging and exhausting. I practiced diligently until I thought I had mastered a phrase. Then I would sally forth with wonderful confidence and wait with happy anticipation for the proper response. But usually all I got were blank stares or an embarrassing "Huh?" indicating that I had missed the tones again.

After language study, I was plopped into an entirely Taiwanese environment with few foreigners in sight. During my initial two years there, I managed to acquire enough Taiwanese to get around and get the gist of simple conversation and sometimes even the outline of a sermon. This accomplishment, however, was no more than a tenuous beginning. Mastery requires a lifetime of arduous study.

Those early months in Taiwan, the land of my calling, retain to this day a cherished place in my memory. After the high drama of God's call, I arrived in Taichung with a heart which had so recently been fallow ground, but now was plowed up deeply into hungrily receptive soil and open as never before to the impulses of the Spirit. The presence of God was very near.

Chapter 19

YUANLIN

Our first crusade was scheduled to begin January 24. Since our team members had arrived somewhat earlier, Rollie suggested that I lead them in preparatory devotional times and Bible studies. I had mixed feelings when I learned that all but one of them were Bible college students now on probation.

I chose to take the team verse by verse through 1 Timothy, Paul's exhortations to a young man, very likely about our age. The boys were attentive and courteous to a fault. Still, three hours of scriptural homiletics taught with the aid of an interpreter of limited gifts can seem like a very long time.

As we planned for the crusade, we decided that mornings would be devoted to street meetings. Various team members would take turns preaching from the elevated back step of the red pickup truck. Thereafter, tracts and gospel portions were to be distributed and efforts made to sell handsomely bound Chinese Bibles and New Testaments. I accompanied Rollie to the local Bible Society warehouse and we loaded our truck with several hundred pounds and thousands of Chinese Scriptures. This was a grand vision, but we were to learn, to our dismay, that Taiwanese people with only limited literacy would not be much inclined to purchase hardback copies of Scriptures which, though reasonably priced, were still for them a considerable investment.

Our initial assignment was in Yuanlin, a city of about thirty thousand located on the main highway one hour south of Taichung. This town was typically steeped in Buddhist, Taoist, and animistic superstition. This conglomeration of beliefs constitutes what scholars call "folk religion."

Yuanlin is one of the island's most fertile areas with dark, rich soil. It produces bumper crops of grain, fruit, and gorgeous roses. The rose gardens are reputed to be among the most beautiful in Asia.

Prior to our arrival, in consultation with church leaders, Rollie had rented a storefront building just a few yards from the main thoroughfare of the city and almost opposite the train station.

Before leaving on the afternoon of January 24, we gathered around the old Ford and bowed our heads in prayer. I was appointed the one and only driver. At this time, few Taiwanese had personal automobiles or a driver's license.

A short time before departure, Rollie informed me that due to unforeseen events he would not be accompanying us on this initial trip. Now I, a novice without language or experience, would be in charge. I was assisted, however, by Pastor Shu, an older gentleman who was given the title of "team captain." Unfortunately, he knew hardly a word of English.

As we approached Yuanlin with Michael, my interpreter, seated beside me and the team members in back atop the baggage and mounds of Bibles, I was keenly aware that for the first time I was leaving the comfortable environs of the OMS compound and missionary family. That night I realized that for me this marked the beginning of a long-term environment change.

Our living quarters proved to be more acceptable than I had anticipated. Taiwan, after a half-century of Japanese rule, though still Chinese, had been manifestly altered in its customs and style of living. Of course, no Western-style beds were provided but simply the typical grass mat tatamis, to which all members of the team were accustomed. I was grateful for my army surplus air mattress, though on occasion it sprang leaks and required patching. Still, it provided this *waiguoren* (foreigner) more than adequate comfort for a good night's sleep.

One unfortunate feature of our quarters was the non-flush hole-in-the-floor toilet, which was situated almost immediately adjacent to my bed behind a thin plywood partition. Two holes in a hopelessly narrow closet-like enclosure served for what in America would be a clean porcelain seat-covered bowl that could be flushed after using.

Ideally, these devices should be cleaned out regularly to prevent undue accumulations and stench. The Taiwanese, however, are not as much offended by foul odors as we pampered Westerners are, and they regarded the cleaning of the commode as something less than imperative. With seven healthy young men using the one facility, the contents piled up, providing a wealth of fertilizer for local crops.

Finally, Rollie complained, and I dared to add my opinion. The proper parties were contacted and arrangements made for regular disposal. Western sanitary values and practices had not yet reached Taiwan, and small children waded gleefully in open sewers.

Screens were few, and the doors left open made an inviting environment for mosquitoes. I was grateful that at night, a large mosquito net was hung over the entire sleeping area. Another inconvenience I soon became aware of related to the matter of removing one's shoes. In Japanese-style tatami homes, it was unthinkable to keep your shoes on. For uninitiated foreigners, this can be tedious business indeed. I finally invested in a pair of slippers and then clopped around our quarters like everyone else.

Two of the team members slept downstairs in a small cubicle that also served as our dining room. The remainder of the ground floor fronted on Tzuyo Lu, which means "Liberty Street." This area had been furnished with simple wooden benches and served as our chapel, which when full would seat about forty.

The first evening we ate at a local restaurant, but afterwards we were mostly at the mercy of the cook whom we had hired. At mealtime, we all sat on the tatami floor mats and crowded around a table sixteen inches high. Average income in Taiwan at this time was approximately the equivalent of fifteen dollars per month. We agreed that the team members would all contribute two hundred N.T. (New Taiwan) dollars, about five dollars each month. Out of this amount the cook would purchase and prepare for us what we hoped would be sufficiently nutritious meals. This was no small challenge.

Her favorite meal consisted of a thin squash soup. Squash, unfortunately, was one of the few vegetables I found nearly impossible to stomach. Along with the soup always came the inevitable cheap rice, which was often garnished with small stones and other extraneous material. On top of this were placed some remnants of pork fat, virtually the only semblance of meat we could afford. The rice was always prepared in sufficient quantities to forestall utter starvation.

The most difficult meal of the day was always breakfast. We were served a bowl of syi-fan (watery rice porridge) with slim rations of peanuts, pickles, and perhaps a slice of bean curd. Lunch included small salted fish along with all sorts of vegetables such as peas, bamboo sprouts, and a bean curd stew.

On occasion, usually Sunday at noon, the entire team would journey to a local Japanese eatery. There I learned to like fermented miso (bean curd) soup, which I had first sampled in Japan and found distasteful, and oyako-donburi, which means "chicken and egg in a bowl."

Now that I was in the company of the team day and night, I learned soon enough the limits of my Taiwanese vocabulary.

I despaired of getting the eight tones right, but the boys appreciated my efforts and praised my "excellent Taiwanese." For communication in my own language, I had to resort to Michael, my interpreter, whose many deficiencies I became increasingly aware of.

At mealtime, Michael was the greatest offender. Always seated close beside me, he took great delight in filling his mouth with rice and then launching into long descriptive sentences that came out of his mouth along with a generous spattering of rice and grotesque noises. Soup is slurped, and everyone slurps. No one bothered to use cups for the tea, which was usually stone cold. It was simply poured into the rice bowl and drunk with relish.

In the initial plan for the crusade, Rollie told me that he was planning on spending a large portion of his time working with us at Yuanlin. This never happened. During the early weeks, he would occasionally join us for several days to help in the initiation of the work.

Since Rollie had hired my interpreter, Michael, he did his utmost to initiate him into his assignment. Rolland had lived in Japan and spoke some Japanese as well as Chinese but not Taiwanese. So he too was dependent on the services of Michael. In the matter of preaching, Michael was hopelessly inept, convincing Rollie that I would likely have no effective speaking ministry.

In the mornings, when we scheduled street meetings, Rollie accompanied us for a time, intent on proving the validity of his vision of evangelizing the island by the sale of thousands of Bibles. After the first few days, in which we distributed many tracts and Bible booklets but sold very few of the Bibles, Rollie came to share our skepticism. Now we were obliged to return to the Bible Society the thousands of Bibles we had initially bought. We hoped they would give us our money back. A few days later this was accomplished, but not without some difficulty.

Still, Rollie's zeal and many virtues were a great encouragement to me. He had a heart as big as the great outdoors, and it was impossible to sustain any hard feelings toward him. I admired the fact that he had a missionary spirit that was not quenched by the often-deadening routine of teaching and administrative work.

Having grown up in Asia where I'd spent much of my early life in boarding school, far from the comforts and security of my parents, I had assumed that my adaptation to another Asian environment would be fairly effortless. But this was not to be.

January is a cold month in Taiwan. We were housed in a facility without heat and with few of the comforts to which I was accustomed. All of this contributed not only to full-fledged culture shock but also to plain old-fashioned homesickness. I soon discovered that adaptation to this environment was by no means an effortless thing. After the initial excitement of arriving and the novelty of "first times," I found myself in desperate need of a kindred spirit in which to confide. The language barrier becomes a wall that prevents much comradeship or fellowship. For the first time in many years, I knew real loneliness. All of this threatened to draw me into a vacuum of despair.

In the midst of all these painful adjustments, however, I began to discover a wonderful solace that I had previously known more in theory than experience. I could not have survived these days without the intimacy of the person of my Savior. He covered me with His wings of mercy and the shadow of the Almighty. Through the ominous clouds of depression had filtered the promises of God, and they refreshed my soul over and over.

As always, when I came to the end of my own resources, the provisions of God took on a fresh reality. The Word and prayer become increasingly alive, giving rise to an insatiable hunger for more of Him.

There was a great task to be accomplished in this city and all was futile without resources and strength. My wisdom was always imperfect and my judgment flawed. Now I was learning that the strongholds of darkness will not prevail against the assault of the gospel when it is empowered by the person of the Holy Spirit.

At this time, I was practically the only foreigner residing in Yuanlin. Several blocks from our quarters, however, lived a very old and infirmed Scandinavian lady. She had spent most of her life in China and was finding the Taiwanese dialect impossible to master. We visited on occasion and prayed together. Despite the apparent futility of her situation, her face was lighted with the wonderful glory that marks older Christians who have walked a lifetime with the Savior. Apart from the two of us, there was only one other foreigner, a Catholic priest from Europe who, unfortunately, seemed to make an effort to avoid association with this insensitive and clueless American.

I found myself transported into an environment so foreign that I felt more than ever like a creature from another world. Some of these rural Taiwanese had never before seen an American in person. Children followed me everywhere, providing me with an entourage of small creatures in my wake. The bolder ones would run up against my leg and greet me with the familiar cry, "Bi-kok-lang! Bi-kok-lang!" which means "American man." The less courteous shouted, "A-to-ka!" which means "big nose" or "hook nose." For the first time in my life, I became self-conscious of my nose, which indeed was almost twice as large as that of the average Taiwanese. I would respond with the words "Phai-ginna" which they knew well enough meant "naughty child."

I had the feeling that I was standing on tiptoes on the edge of what for me would spell a new era, facing daily a chasm of the unknown and untried. Yet I was excited with all the prospects spread out before me. I was thrilled with the positive manifestations of God on my behalf, things that assured me beyond any doubt that He had brought me to Taiwan and had set before me a task of immeasurable joy and blessing.

CHAPTER 20

A MINISTRY BEGUN

We soon commenced our regular evening activities. First came the children's service, announced by the beating of the big drum, which drew children from every quarter of the city until the gospel hall was packed with small bodies. A large banner on which were inscribed simple gospel choruses was raised, and the youngsters screamed out, "Come to Jesus! Come to Jesus!" in unison. This was followed by a Bible story illustrated with slides. Then followed the adult service, again heralded by the big bass drum. Our team members fanned out along the streets adjacent to the hall inviting passersby to the meeting. The first week or two a good number were drawn out of curiosity. This scene was quite amazing, an American living and working among them and even eating Taiwanese food. Most of them had never witnessed such a thing.

During the following weeks, however, we discerned a troubling pattern. Now that the residents of the town had determined that the foreigner and his friends were not dangerous, they were no longer very interested in what we were doing. Soon, to our dismay, only a few were attending the adult services. This called for earnest prayer, lengthy morning intercession all focused on the plea, "Lord, send the people." For some reason I had assumed that the presence of a foreigner and the spiritual hunger of the people would guarantee us crowds – if not great crowds, at least small crowds. But now the opposite seemed to be happening.

The third week, after we had completed our morning prayers, my colleagues alarmed me with a shocking suggestion. "Mr. Erny, why don't you open an English class? Young people have a very strong urge to learn English. And they have never had a teacher who speaks English as his mother tongue. If you will just teach English, good numbers of young people will attend."

"But God has called me to preach the gospel. I have no interest in teaching English." More than this, I was all too aware of my ignorance of English grammar. Any questions on that subject would leave me frozen with embarrassment. I was emphatic. I was not in Taiwan to teach English!

Still, things were not improving; in fact, they were going from bad to worse. And, with Michael as my interpreter, my preaching was an ordeal. With the decreasing attendance came an even more urgent plea that I teach English. I agreed to try. I felt sure that a single class would spell the end of my English teaching. We scheduled the first class for the following Wednesday afternoon at three o'clock. Stephen Teh, who had artistic gifts, fashioned a prominent and carefully lettered poster which he attached to the entryway. "An American, Mr. Erny," it announced, would be the teacher. I was totally unprepared for what was just ahead.

That Wednesday, after my afternoon nap, I descended the narrow staircase from our sleeping quarters to the chapel below. What greeted me was quite beyond my expectation or even imagination. The small hall was absolutely packed with young people as well as an assortment of elderly ladies and gentlemen. Our chapel could not accommodate them all. They were standing outside, clustered about the entryway. Fortunately, the team members, whose faith far exceeded mine, had come prepared with registration blanks. Some applicants were weeded out for one reason or another but when registration was finished, I found that I was facing a most fearful prospect of teaching some thirty to forty eager students.

With Michael's help, I explained the schedule and the purpose of the course: to help them with their English and to also explain the good news of Jesus.

Now I pondered the fact that for teaching materials in the English language we had nothing other than King James Bibles. The English in the King James Bible had not been in vogue since the seventeenth century. I soon learned that using this ancient tongue as a text for teaching twentieth-century English was not logical. Apologetically, I muddled through that first week and by the next week had procured some suitable English materials. A number of those early students gave up in disgust and departed.

There remained, however, about twenty or so mostly high school and university students. This was possible because during the long Chinese New Year's holiday, most students returned home. Before long, I became well acquainted with my eager pupils and friendships flourished. Many of the students started attending the evening services and amazingly one by one raised their hands acknowledging their desire to receive Christ as Savior. Among these who responded were several members of the Chang family who had been prominent in Yuanlin for generations. During the Japanese era, they had owned a lumber business and sizable portions of land and housing in the very center of the city.

The first of this family to come to Christ was Chang Hong Dau, who was an English major studying in a Presbyterian college in the capital city of Taipei. I little dreamed how God was to use this young man. He would become a lifelong friend as well as a beloved colleague in our future radio ministry. Some years later I asked him to write his testimony, which follows.

I heard the gospel several times during my college days but for the following reasons I refused to consider Christianity:

First, I was born and raised in a Taiwanese family that worshiped and served the traditional religion. A large upper portion of our house was set aside as a shrine for idols and memorial tablets for my ancestors. Just as I was taught the tradition of this religion, I was expected to pass on this knowledge to my descendants. Since Christians do not worship their ancestors, my people believe that Christians shamefully neglect their filial duty. Therefore, I reasoned that if I became a Christian I would be scorned by my family for abandoning my historical, cultural, and religious heritage. I certainly did not want that to happen.

Secondly, I learned from my study of history that China had been cruelly invaded by Westerners who forced the Chinese to submit to what are now called the notorious "unequal treaties." Since missionaries had come to China about this same time, the Chinese came to view the Western religion as a tool used by Europeans to invade China and overturn her politics and culture. Thus, Christianity was a partner in the facilitation of these abuses.

During my college days, I had on occasion attended evangelistic services in a nearby church. Before each meeting, a few believers would beat on large drums to draw the crowds. One evening they practically forced me to enter the church and listen to the message. Once inside I noticed that older people made up the majority of the audience. Moreover, I could hardly understand what the pastor was saying. After that, I avoided churches and, whenever I heard the threatening sound of drums, I would take another route.

In 1959, I was home for the winter vacation when I discovered that a church team led by a young American missionary had come to Yuanlin and opened an English class. I was majoring in English and planned to teach the language when I graduated. I even dreamed of someday serving overseas as an ambassador. I wanted to showcase the culture and pride of the Chinese people to Western countries, so I considered the opportunity to improve my English by actually conversing with this American missionary. Of course, I would never convert to his religion, and I was reluctant to make friends with these proud, superior Americans.

One day, however, as I passed the small gospel church, I saw a young foreigner dressed in simple clothes. He was bent down wiping mud from a vehicle. This humble task is something that no upper-class Chinese would ever do. The scene shocked me. I had earlier seen GIs in Taipei, and they always impressed me as being proud and aloof, but here this young man, instead of living lavishly like those GIs, had actually left his home in wealthy America and come to a village in Taiwan to work, even sleeping on the floor. This made a deep impression and encouraged my desire to learn English from him.

I joined the small class studying the Bible with Mr.

Erny every afternoon. At the end of each session, he smiled, shook our hands, and invited us to the evening gospel meeting. Because the English lessons were free, I thought that I ought to at least show my appreciation by accepting his invitation. So in the evening I went to the evangelistic center, sat on a hard bench, and listened to the speaker's message. Those messages moved and convinced me of my need of a Savior. I finally confessed my sins publicly, repented, and accepted Jesus as my personal Savior. Jesus' forgiveness and salvation completely transformed my life.

Although I was becoming better acquainted with this student, an unusually sincere young man, I had no idea of what was transpiring in his mind and heart. After our English class one afternoon, he asked me if we could talk. I recall that we walked together through the streets in the heart of the city.

His first words to me were "I want you to know that I have decided to become a Christian. I must follow Jesus." This was stunning. This kind of thing happening so abruptly and his publicly proclaiming acceptance of Christ, as well as his rejection of the idolatrous Buddhist faith, were rare indeed. I was not convinced that he actually understood the implications of what he was saying.

"Have you thought this through carefully?" I asked. "Are you sure that you want to believe?"

"Oh, yes," he said. "I am sure. I must become a Christian. I have decided to follow Christ." When I inquired into his background and the circumstances which had led him to this decision, he told me that he came from one of the leading families in the town. His grandfather was, at one time, the mayor of Yuanlin. In spite of these benefits, wealth, and fame,

Mr. Chang said, "We have never been happy." He then told me of the frequent conflicts that rage in many large and wealthy families. He spoke of a male cousin and the envy and hatred that had developed between them. Added to this was what he called a great number of unresolved issues between members of the family.

"When I accepted Jesus," he continued, "it was as though a huge rock had been rolled off my back. The heavy burden of hate that I have been carrying for the past twelve years has been removed from my heart."

After hearing the young man's testimony, I said, "Mr. Chang, you are the first and only Christian in your family. It is inevitable that you will be facing times of testing, perhaps persecution. For this reason I am going to name you Daniel. He is one of the great heroes of the Bible. For his faith, he was cast into a den of lions. Now you also will be, in fact, in a kind of den of lions."

Others in Daniel's family began attending the English classes and the evening services. His aunt, an attractive Japanese lady, had married his uncle during the war years. Upon hearing the gospel, she almost immediately opened her heart to Christ and, though she never learned much English, she soon became one of our closest friends and supporters. Her excitement in her newfound faith was palpable. She was transformed by a baptism of joy. Her daughter, whom we later named Ruth, joined Daniel as one of our most faithful students. Her quiet demeanor at first gave us no inkling of her unusual mind and gifts, gifts that would one day be used for the glory of God. After Ruth opened her heart to Christ, she eagerly witnessed to both her brother and her father. She shared the gospel with so much love and persistence that her father was wonderfully converted.

Ruth would later graduate from our Bible seminary and immigrate to the United States, coming as a student to Azusa

College in California and then Asbury Seminary, and later receiving a master of education degree from Columbia University in New York. She eventually settled in the New York area where she became a leader in a local Chinese church. Now, for the most part of each year she returns to Taiwan and is a professor in the OMS-founded Chung Tai Theological Seminary in Taichung and is also a gifted writer and speaker who regularly leads retreats.

In the ensuing years, one by one, almost every member of Daniel and Ruth's family came to faith in Christ. The one exception was Daniel's older brother, who by tradition inherited the leadership and decision-making rights in the Chang clan. He became a notorious gambler and, though very gifted, squandered much of the family wealth. For fifteen years, while Daniel and I met together for weekly prayer, we always prayed for this apparently hopeless older brother. He had absolutely refused to even listen to Daniel's presentation of the gospel. Toward the end, however, his habit of chewing betel nut had resulted in cancer of the mouth. In the hospital, unable to speak and given only a short time to live, he listened and even welcomed Daniel's witness and accepted Jesus. I had the privilege of speaking at his funeral.

I cannot complete this story without mention of Daniel's grandmother, a lifelong idol worshiper, who had turned a large upstairs room into a kind of shrine, complete with images and ancestral tablets. For years, she viewed Daniel and Ruth and the others as traitors to the family heritage and refused their attempts to share the gospel with her. Now, nearly ninety years of age, she found that she was dying. Her Buddhist faith provided no solace and she was increasingly distraught. For all her zeal, she had no peace.

Finally, in desperation, she allowed both Daniel and Ruth to share the gospel with her. Through their witness, she accepted

Jesus. Though feeble, she went to the shrine on the second floor of the house and burned three incense sticks to the gods and said good-bye to each of them. Then she burned the images as she declared that she was now trusting in the true and living God and His Son Jesus.

When we returned to Taiwan in 1964, I discovered that Daniel, Ruth, and other members of the family were the mainstays of the church in Yuanlin. Daniel gave up the lucrative English school he had founded in Yuanlin and became my colleague in our Taichung Bible seminary. Then together we pioneered a nationwide evangelistic ministry, a daily teaching of English and the gospel on a major radio network. This ministry continued for fifteen years.

During those terrible days when I was struggling against God's call to the crusade, I could never have imagined how glorious and extensive would be the fruit of my simple obedience. Daniel is the most persistent witness that I have ever known. I cannot begin to name all who have come to Christ through his witness, preaching, teaching, and interpreting. God continues to use Daniel and his family.

The owners of the building in which our team was residing had a prosperous bookstore and were also named Chang. We found their hearts open to the gospel and members of the family attended our meetings. Their three sons, John, Samuel, and Paul, all accepted Christ. I was often in their home but something puzzled me. Every time my presence was announced, it produced gales of laughter. What was this all about? I finally learned that in Japanese, the language which they all spoke, the word *oni*, which is as close as they could come to the name Erny, means "devil." So my introduction was always an announcement that the Devil had come!

One noon as we ate together in their home, John, the most

congenial of the boys, leaned across the table and said, "This is a most happy day, one we will always remember."

Then Samuel added, "Before you came, I did not like Americans but now I've changed my mind." This family eventually immigrated to Australia.

As the English classes grew, I accumulated a special society of Chinese friends. Everyone who received Christ was given a Bible name in English. Young people on that leaf-shaped island found themselves in a common vacuum. In their changing world, the old vestiges of their ancient religions seemed no longer tenable. This generation was becoming aware of the increasing influence of the Western world. More and more of them dreamed of someday going to the States. Today a good number of my former English class students are American citizens and remain true to their Christian faith.

So surprisingly successful and gratifying was this first English class that thereafter it became a primary means and mainstay of our ministry in Taiwan. Learning English is sometimes called the golden key. Most Asians who have mastered English are assured lifetime employment in some of the world's best companies. Parents, realizing the tremendous advantage of English fluency, go to great lengths to introduce their children to foreigners and impress upon them the importance of studying this most difficult language with native speakers.

CHAPTER 21

TOULIU

After three months, our Yuanlin crusade was coming to a close. The Taiwan Holiness Church leaders had investigated other cities still without a church. They decided that our next assignment would be Touliu, which means "six bushels." It was a small town of perhaps twenty thousand and is situated across a large river spanned by the longest bridge on the island.

But shortly before our move to Touliu came a signal event that was to deeply bless and influence my entire two-year mission in Taiwan. Earlier we had been visited by a Presbyterian missionary engaged in rural evangelism. He applauded all that we were attempting to do. After I had spoken one evening, laboring mightily to accomplish something of value in spite of interpreter Michael's constant stuttering and mistranslations, he sidled up to me and whispered, "Ed, Michael has got to go."

Later when I mentioned this comment to Rollie, he wholeheartedly agreed. Within days, Michael had been gently and kindly released for whatever calling God might have for him. During the interval that followed, we were energized and blessed by the translation services of Joseph Wang, the very talented son of our church superintendent, John Wang.

Joseph was a graduate of Taiwan's top university where he majored in engineering. He now felt called into the ministry and had made plans to attend Asbury Theological Seminary.

His plans, however, were constantly deterred by the fact that he was still recovering from tuberculosis, so travel to the U.S. was postponed. During this interval, OMS decided to ask this young man with a near-perfect understanding of English and true Christian zeal to assist the crusade in Touliu.

With the coming of Joseph, the whole atmosphere of our mission was wonderfully improved. Now, preaching, which had been such a struggle for me, was greatly enhanced both linguistically and spiritually. As it worked out, the clearance from the Department of Health to go abroad coincided with the very time my mission in Taiwan would be completed. Thus for a year and a half, Joseph and I were true comrades and coworkers. He was an invaluable instrument of God for preaching the gospel to the Chinese and bringing many to the foot of the cross.

Today Dr. Wang is a well-known Chinese theological scholar and evangelist. He served on the faculty of Asbury Seminary for many years and speaks often at Chinese conferences in the U.S. and abroad. He also assisted in the translation of the New King James Bible.

We had not been in Touliu long before we were asking what it was that had induced our church leaders to send us to this squalid, degenerate location for the next three or four months. To my foreign nose, this town seemed plagued by foul odors. It was also strewn with filth and inhabited by, what seemed to me, a degenerate class of people, the wreckage of centuries of satanic darkness.

Our gospel hall and sleeping quarters were located in the heart of the city, almost adjacent to a shabby market place. We moved in on a Friday. Our sleeping area was actually larger than that of Yuanlin, but this virtue did little to alleviate the filth and heat that assailed us. Our quarters had not been furnished with an electric fan and, sandwiched between two old city buildings, we were bereft of any passing breeze. The place retained the stifling heat long after the merciless sun set behind the maze of shacks and rice fields. Trying to sleep on the broad tatami mat floor, I found great beads of sweat trickling down my limbs. But I had grown up in India, I told myself, and had experienced heat before.

There were also flies. Since our quarters had no screens, the pestilential creatures poured in through openings in the doors and windows. They came at us relentlessly, buzzing happily over our bodies. In the afternoons, our habitual naps were really impossible. Their companions, the mosquitoes, invaded at night with a viciousness that I had seldom experienced. One of my feet, which had somehow edged out from underneath the mosquito net, became disfigured with four or five nice fat welts that set me scratching the rest of the night.

Perhaps the worst feature of our quarters was that the dwelling reposed above a sewer, and through the generous cracks in the floorboards we could see large rats scuttling back and forth day and night.

Our crude kitchen was equipped with a charcoal stove, and uncovered food made a perfect haven for cockroaches. Only a few of the creatures appeared during the day but once the sun set it was high carnival time. One night when I needed a glass of water, I extricated myself from the mosquito net and made my way to the kitchen. When I turned on the light, it was as though the entire room was set in motion. What was all this frenzied movement? As I came to life and my eyes focused, I perceived there were a hundred or more (I counted them) hungry cockroaches in earnest quest of their evening repast. What a sight!

When missionaries got together and regaled one another with accounts of their sufferings for the Lord featuring dealing with sundry pests, my cockroach story always topped them all.

Our diet in Touliu was, if anything, worse than Yuanlin. For the most part, meal times during the crusade were the only time in my life when I dreaded the dinner bell. Meals were something to be endured. One effect of all this was that I lost weight. Some expressed concern about this, but I continued to enjoy good and vigorous health.

To supplement our meager diet, in the evenings after our evangelistic meetings had ended, we would often seek out street vendors for some tasty noodles. A small bowl would cost no more than a few cents. The chopsticks, of course, were never clean. To prepare the utensils for the next customer, the vendor simply sloshed the bowl and chopsticks in a wooden bucket full of tepid gray water, which he kept under the counter. As a precaution, we would dip the chopsticks in boiling water before eating. Why every one of us did not die of hepatitis is still a mystery.

The following day added to our discomfort as traffic stirred up clouds of dust from the unpaved street just outside our front door, and gradually a dirty grey film settled over everything. Baths were of small benefit and, as for bathing facilities, we were furnished an open cement patch outside the back door and a bucket.

Here also was the outhouse. The place was a shock to sundry human senses. In addition to the malodorous assault, small worms had attached themselves to feces and seemed to be multiplying in number before our eyes. They took the form of chubby white maggots. This writhing mass of life gave the receptacle pit the appearance of a boiling cauldron. The fact that our backyard was mutually accessible to our neighbors did nothing to make the necessity of a trip to the outhouse less unpleasant.

Western-style toilets in Asia, which at that time were mostly for the benefit of foreigners, are often called water closets and are identified by the initials "W.C." Mr. Teh, our artist, created a large sign for the outhouse door. The fancy "W.C." on the door he designated as the "Washington Club" for my benefit.

The shared backyard had also become a repository for all manner of discarded articles: broken jars, straw for chickens, decrepit articles of furniture, and scraps of corrugated metal.

Added to these delights was the company of the neighborhood rooster. He began his joyful chorus with gusto at sun-up every morning and often entertained us during the afternoon naptime as though inspired by some evil power intent on depriving the tired preacher boys of their slumber.

In typical fashion, wherever we lodged we shared a common, very thin wall with our neighbors on both sides of us. We overheard many heated conversations being carried on with great vehemence. Some of our neighbors were involved in familial warfare on a daily basis.

Later, when residing in Hualien, it became apparent that one of our female neighbors had serious mental problems. Long soliloquies would give way to screaming, which in time evolved into continuous weeping and wailing, great shrill cries in the late afternoon and evening.

Well, I thought, for the first time this is real missionary life. But what of it? I was healthy, well, strong, and even nourished by three red and green vitamin pills a day. Flies and mosquitoes could be screened out as well as some of the dust. I even convinced the field committee that a small expenditure for both electric fans and screens would not be an unpardonable extravagance. We were soon to learn that physical discomforts and inconveniences were child's play compared to the onslaught of satanic influence.

That first week we proceeded to launch our street meetings. For this we had obtained permission and the required documents from the city authorities. Our favorite location was the crowded market area during early morning, the busiest time of the day. We would first arrange the loudspeaker atop the truck. I situated myself directly opposite with a bundle of tracts in my hands, thrusting them politely at the streams of people passing by on foot, bicycles, or pedicabs usually full of groceries or even a live pig.

Things went rather well. Brother Tan would take hold of the mike and sing out in a bold voice, "Lai sin Iaso hen chai!" (Come to Jesus right now!) An audience would begin to form. Brother Loa would place Bibles for sale on a table. Another team member unrolled the gospel charts. His favorite was "The sinner's dream," describing the terrors of a lost soul.

The crowd would usually grow, especially in places where foreigners were seldom seen. Sometimes a fight would erupt between street hawkers vying for an advantageous position. Obviously, the people had never heard anything of this sort before. Prospects for preaching the gospel were encouraging.

Some mornings, halfway through the meeting, men in black uniforms with their officious gait and protruding lower lips would appear. "Hey, what's going on here?" they would demand.

Joseph, less intimidated than the others and with an air of self-confidence, stepped forward and explained, "We have already gained approval from the police office."

"So does that allow you to block the traffic?" came the reply. "Get out of here and make it fast."

Sometimes the sound of the policeman's belligerent roar was a greater drawing card than the message which, incidentally, was going on at the same time with Brother Tan preaching.

Once while in Hualien, we witnessed a curious phenomenon. The simple Taiwanese, our audience, were of their own free will siding with us against our tormentors, causing the infuriated officer to depart in a huff.

I remember, however, that although this first week in Touliu was in many ways one of the hardest times of my life, I was, as the poet says, "sustained and soothed by an unfaltering trust," a true gift from the Lord. How could I ever forget the opening evening service? Of course, the foreigner was billed as the speaker. Everyone agreed that this would be a good opening for the campaign.

The chapel was well-enough filled but that was the only encouraging aspect of the entire evening. Everything went wrong. The singing was terrible, the participation almost nil, the prayer turned out to be a tiring discourse, and the special musical number was impaired by numerous disruptions.

I was convinced that the sermon I had carefully prepared would be received by an attentive audience. The message, however, which I had previously used with satisfaction, seemed to fall apart. I had a stifling sense of the presence of Satan, more than I had ever known. I lost my train of thought, and I sincerely wished I were elsewhere.

Then the congregation began to leave, not in ones or twos, but a general scattering, and I hadn't even finished preaching. Children wandered up and down the aisles, and people chattered merrily. Others stood at the entranceway talking noisily. I preached on, if what I was doing could even be called preaching. At the end of the message, my invitation was greeted with a few blank stares and a near total lack of interest.

That night I went to bed dejected but vaguely aware that God was trying to speak to me. Most awfully was I conscious of the fact that Satan was a resident patron and inhabitant of this fair city of Touliu. Almost all of the services that week appeared to be time wasted and a repetition of that first one.

I sensed stirrings of discontent among the boys. What had possessed our captain, Brother Shu, to rent for us this infuriating and depressing residence? But what disturbed us most was the class of people that our services seemed to attract. Not at all like Yuanlin. These folk seemed degenerate and perverse. The children wandered urchin-like up and down the aisles. Two of the older ones got in a fight. This brought only casual admonitions from indifferent mothers, one of whom was nursing an infant at her breast. Some were determined to smoke despite our no-smoking signs.

One night a drunken fellow wandered into the hall and, after inquiring in a wavering voice what our business was, promptly went to sleep with his chin dropped on his chest. But he did not continue his slumbers for long. In mid-service, he woke up and casually urinated on the floor to the disgust and annoyance of everyone.

After gratifying successes in Yuanlin, the humiliating failure of our first attempt in Touliu was depressing indeed. The team would gather after the evening service to discuss and analyze our problems. Some blamed the location, insisting that the class of people in this part of town was not easily able to comprehend the gospel or our preaching. Others said the crowds were of a transient nature and were not accustomed to sitting through religious services, something Buddhists seldom had. But the facts were plain to all of us – we were failures.

We prayed, but our earnest petitions seemed attended by fatigue and listlessness. Yet, gradually, through the disappointment and despair, I began to feel something like the dawn of a celestial sunrise, as though we were nearing the peak of a very difficult and stubborn mountain.

Chapter 22

"YE SHALL BEAR FRUIT"

Reading in my Bible one evening I was arrested by 1 Peter 1:6-7 which reads: *though now for a season, if need be, ye are in heaviness through manifold temptations: That the trial of your faith, being much more precious than of gold that perisheth, though it be tried by fire, might be found unto the praise and honour and glory at the appearing of Jesus Christ* (KJV). This message gradually swept over me with a gratifying intensity.

Attendance at the evening evangelistic services began to grow. A young fellow wandered into the hall half-drunk one night. He was unshaven and glassy-eyed. He came back again the following night and stayed after to make a decision. He had an unusual story. In his early life, he had had some church influence and then turned from all of it to claim atheism. Lately, things had not been going well. His thoughts had reverted to God. That night when he heard the message his heart was troubled. Later, he found it impossible to sleep. He was back again the following night, and our team became a friend to him.

Down the block was a store selling pots, pans, and household goods. I stopped there to pick up a wastebasket. They had no wastebaskets, but the man who waited on us was obviously educated. He addressed me in English so I gave him my card and invited him to the hall. The next night he was there. I learned that his father was the proprietor of the store and he himself was the English teacher in the local high school. The following night he brought his principal to the meeting. Afterward, I walked home with him. It was a wonderful opportunity to explain the way of salvation. Before we concluded our campaign, he received Christ as Savior.

Of course, I lost no time in instituting the afternoon English Bible classes. God had been using these so powerfully to attract numbers of youth and the more educated members of the community. I had been working on a textbook in bilingual format entitled *Twenty Lessons from the Life of Christ*. The little booklet proved very popular, created considerable interest, and drew our students back every afternoon to learn more of the miracle-working Jesus.

I would start each class with a simple gospel song. My favorite was "I've got the joy, joy, joy, joy down in my heart." I remember a shy, thin postman dressed in his wrinkled green uniform and so obviously self-conscious that I guessed he would never be back for another session. But he returned. We shook hands. I felt a strong love for the frightened young man. He looked a bit incredulous that anyone, especially a foreigner, would ever take an interest in him.

Saturday afternoon during my prayer hour, I was strongly conscious of the presence of the Lord. As had happened before, it seemed to break suddenly upon me, enduing me with a kind of energy, a fire. I rose from my knees, inwardly calmed, and what the Bible calls *stayed on thee*.

Immediately I heard someone at the front door of the chapel. It was one of the fellows who had been attending my English Bible class. Stumblingly and a bit embarrassed, he inquired about the way of salvation. He was not sure of the terminology or what he should ask for but there was eagerness in his manner. He said, "You must explain the story of the Bible to me." I couldn't believe my ears. My soul began to take off on me and bear me far beyond that shabby little town of Touliu. We sat down with bilingual Bibles and heaven settled right around us.

I rejoiced in the sweet task which I found to be the most gratifying a mortal can know – that of pointing a hungry soul to the Savior. With his limited English and my inadequate Taiwanese, we read together passage after passage. When we were through, we bowed our heads and prayed. That afternoon the young man became a child of God.

I named him John, John Li. He came back several afternoons after that for further instruction. I have known few new Christians so hungry, so very famished for something that satisfies. Not long after, John, who was in the military, was dispatched to another location.

He had no sooner left, however, than another gentleman, very courteous and slightly older, in similar khaki military uniform appeared. He was likewise eager to know the Word of God. I named him James. He told me that for years he had been seeking the true way of life, even dutifully trying to pray and read the Bible. He had found it dull and meaningless. He knew that there must be something more. How could he get it? I turned to Romans chapter 7 with its story of trial and failure, then on to triumph in chapter 8, noting the repetition of the words *in Christ*.

James was a part of Chiang Kai-shek's army who had been forced to leave parents, relatives, and all that was familiar to flee to Taiwan in 1949. He had some medical skills and served as kind of a male nurse in the local hospital. In these days, tuberculosis was the most virulent and relentless of killers. Several wards in the hospital were devoted to men in the final stages of this cruel disease.

Through James, I found an open door to the military hospital. No preaching was permitted in army camps and quarters. However, the first day I went to the hospital with James, no one with authority was present. James insisted that I follow him through the wards and preach a simple gospel message to these men who had but a short time to live. We went from ward to ward, delivering brief, impromptu sermons and enrolling some patients in a Bible correspondence course.

My friendship with James continued to grow. He introduced me to a number of military friends and local acquaintances. He was a relentless witness and seldom appeared at our chapel without a friend or acquaintance in tow. God had sent him as a special encouragement to me. He proved a dear and lasting friend. I kept in touch with him for some time after my return to the U.S.

One evening I was scheduled to speak in the evangelistic service. What a glorious night! I didn't notice the abominable acoustics and hardly a person walked out. The usual street noise seemed almost lulled into reverence.

The chief of police was in the front row with his wife. He listened intently. A number of students from my English class were present. When the invitation was given, four raised their hands, indicating their desire to receive Christ. That night seemed to mark the beginning of what would be a glorious outpouring of God's Spirit in Touliu.

At another evening service, an English teacher sat toward the back of the hall. She was dressed immaculately. I later learned that she was fifty, but no one would have guessed her to be more than thirty-five. She had about her that gentle quality and courtesy that is so often evident in cultured Chinese.

Yet she was sad. When she was not forcing a smile, she allowed an emptiness of face to betray her true feelings. She too was hungry. It was the kind of hunger that bespeaks years of pain and disappointment. Clearly she longed to believe but somehow couldn't. "Is it true that this man Jesus can really calm a storm?" she asked. And then, "No, I cannot believe. I do not know if there is a God." Finally, however, her terrible longing to believe began to overcome the lingering doubts. Then it happened, first with little ripples of hope, then faith, and finally torrents of joy.

The house-to-house gospel distribution was always a part of our crusade schedule. In the afternoon, the boys produced their map and charted their course of distribution while I taught the English class.

After some weeks of street meetings in Touliu, we decided to target outlying areas. Since my white face excited great curiosity, the team insisted that I do most of the preaching. Each day we would travel to remote villages, stationing ourselves in market places that were busy with people during early hours. The PA system belted out simple melodies and invitations to hear the good news. Then I would perch on the back step of the truck and preach with Joseph interpreting. A crowd would immediately form. Sometimes as many as two hundred would throng the truck, listening intently.

We passed out tracts and Bible booklets and also enrolled scores of the more literate in a free Bible correspondence course published by The Evangelical Alliance Mission. A tract that I had written had an attached tear-off sheet for readers to respond to, requesting a free New Testament and also a visit from one of our team members. Almost every day produced a number of responses. This made the afternoon visitation work far easier and more effective.

Among our street crowds were often children, especially during the summer months when they were out of school. Most of them were friendly but some had a decidedly mischievous streak. One day as I mingled among the crowd passing out tracts, a small fellow came behind me and took delight in pinching me on the back of my thigh. When I did not respond in anger, it encouraged him to do it again, only more intensely. By now

I was annoyed, and the next time the lad appeared I reached down and retaliated with a vigorous pinch of my own. This sent the lad screaming in protest of cruel mistreatment by the American. However, I received no more pinches.

Toward the end of our campaign in Touliu, it was agreed that our energetic labors should be rewarded with a brief holiday. We were not far from the main Chiayi station where one could take a narrow-gauge railroad which, due to the benefit of endless switchbacks, made its way up a steep mountain to the famous Alishan resort. Our destination at the top of the mountain was marked by a huge tree, almost as large as some of the Sequoia redwoods in northern California. But the greatest attraction of Alishan is the fact that if one rose early in the morning and climbed to a lookout point, he could see the famous sea of clouds. This much-touted splendor was a favorite attraction for every visitor.

After securing permission from the field committee, we bought our tickets, boarded the train, and wound our way to the peak where we had lodgings in a comfortable hotel. The next morning we were up at four and after an hour's strenuous walk to the famed lookout point, waited expectantly for the appearance of the sea of clouds. Disappointingly, nothing of the sort appeared. We were told that unfortunately, it was not a good day for viewing this wonder but hopefully next time we would be luckier.

One of the great trials to my intolerant nature came from a member of our team designated as the future pastor of the church that we were planting in Touliu. After our team moved on, he and his family would remain. Disconcertingly, we soon learned that this man, given his exalted status, was slow to take suggestions or directions from anyone, including our team leader, Mr. Shu, and me. While the rest of the team rose at 6:30 a.m. for devotions, Mr. Pan slept until 7:00 or later in the bungalow behind the hall occupied by him and his family. His excuse was that since he got to bed later and worked harder, he needed more rest.

My patience was also tried by Caleb, a team member who had been appointed as my future interpreter if and when Joseph left for the United States. In order to permit Caleb to bone up on his very limited English, he was given almost no afternoon visitation assignments.

Caleb, however, abused this interpreter position privilege and for the most part spent the time doing as he pleased, enjoying various pastimes but virtually never studying English. This provoked some verbal admonition on my part, which in the end accomplished nothing. Providentially, Joseph's x-rays for tuberculosis again came back suspect, and his visa was once more denied. Thus, what ordinarily would have been a regrettable turn of events turned out to be a blessing.

Despite the joy and success of the English ministry, in the early days of the crusade there was not a lot about the evening evangelistic services to encourage us.

Following the initial season of dryness, God's spirit broke upon us with unusual joy and fruitfulness. Our small hall filled to overcrowding at night. The people listened and stayed after for counseling. It was a lesson to me that often in the Lord's work when things seem most discouraging and our spirits most despondent, God is preparing for a glorious breakthrough.

Our farewell meeting on July 3 was a gracious time. Mildred Rice made a special trip by train to be with us for the occasion. She had a wonderful gift of enlivening the atmosphere with her happy spirit and barrage of chatter, witticisms, running commentary, and observations. I think the motivation of her visit was to be able to give a firsthand report to my mother, one of her dearest friends, on her son's activities.

Chapter 23

TAINAN AND BEYOND

At this time, we were informed that our next crusade would be in Tainan where our denomination had its mother church. It had been founded during the Japanese occupation, which lasted from 1895 until 1945, and was pastored by probably the most esteemed of all of our clergymen, Pastor Gao. By the time I arrived, he was in his seventies and an invalid.

His colleague was a somewhat younger man known to me as Pastor Lennie Lei. Now with Pastor Gao indisposed, Lei had been elevated to the pastorate of our largest and most influential church. He had a reputation as being a man hard to work with. Moreover, since he had spent so much time in Japan, he was far more fluent in Japanese than in Taiwanese. This in itself was cause for some complaint. Now while assisting the Tainan area churches, we were more or less under the direct control of Pastor Lei.

Our first assignment was to help plant a daughter church in another area of Tainan. The agreed-upon location of this new church was a small rental in a sparsely occupied part of the city. Although there was some fruit from our efforts, the campaign never quite fulfilled expectations. In the last week remaining to us, it was agreed that we would hold evangelistic services in the mother church with the American, of course, featured as the main speaker.

I had previously visited and worshiped in this large church and sensed a troubling coldness. As I prayed, I felt the Lord leading me to preach on the matters of repentance, confession of sin, and the filling of the Holy Spirit. For the first two nights, the house was nearly filled. After that, we noticed curiously and atypically that once the service had begun, no additional people ever entered the hall.

This seemed a strange and unlikely phenomenon. Toward the end of the week, our team members confided that Pastor Lei was unhappy with my preaching, which he said inferred that some of the members might not be born again. This, the pastor told us, made the church look bad. As a result, once the service had begun he had personally locked all the front doors and entryways to the church. Notwithstanding his attempts to undermine our efforts, there were souls at the altar every night.

It was at this time that someone sent me a copy of C.S. Lewis's *Surprised by Joy*. I was already acquainted with Lewis through his imaginative and powerful *The Screwtape Letters*. This new book, really his autobiography, made a terrific impact upon me. That a don from Cambridge and Oxford actually believed in the evangelical faith and had been born again was practically unheard of. Lewis was now unashamedly a lover of the Word of God and all the precious doctrines that were pooh-poohed for the most part by the religious intelligentsia.

This set my soul afire with a new vision for evangelism. In the years that followed, I was careful to read every one of Lewis's books, including the Narnia tales and the somewhat difficult and obscure volumes such as *The Pilgrim's Regress* and *The Problem of Pain*.

With our assignment in Tainan completed, soon we were packing the red truck and charting our route to our next destination, Hualien. We would travel south, half the length of Taiwan to the large city of Kaohsiung and from there wend our way around the southern tip of the island and begin our northward journey to Hualien on the east coast. This would be a long, tedious trip, made more difficult by the fact that recent floods had damaged much of the highway and some of the railway.

We had agreed to leave from Taichung just after the Double Ten celebration. October 10 is the equivalent of the American July 4. This date in 1911 marked the start of a revolution that freed the Chinese nation from millennia of domination by multiple dynasties. This freedom movement was instigated and organized by Sun Yat-sen with General Chiang Kai-shek leading the Nationalists' army and defeating China's many warlords, unifying the nation under one government.

We left that day in a festive spirit. Friends stood by to assure us of their prayers and give us a benediction. The truck was heavily loaded, and I noticed before long that the temperature gauge had reached "H" with the radiator starting to boil. Presently we located the trouble, a broken fan belt. We found an auto parts store, and the proprietor located a fan belt of suitable size – no small task. It was dusk by the time we got on the main highway again. A beautiful sunset silhouetted a couple of ornate temples close by. I stopped momentarily to take pictures.

Driving in Taiwan was quite different from cruising along Route 66 in the U.S. There were at that time so few cars and trucks that farmers and workmen often walked close to the center of the road. At midday, laborers would sprawl on the edge of the pavement for a nap. Bicyclists weaved in and out, around and all over the road, contending with ox carts and pedestrians. Many bicycles were loaded high with grain or a live pig and were wheeled along the side of the road. Traveling over thirty miles per hour was almost suicidal.

The problems were accentuated at night. According to the law, every vehicle must have a light, but this law, like many others in Taiwan, was more often ignored than kept. Moreover, the lumbering army trucks heedlessly crowded their way down the road and were probably responsible for a large percentage of the highway accidents. They were seldom properly lighted with only one headlight working. Worse were the three-wheeled pedicabs and bicycles that in the evenings seemed to melt into the shadows, all but obscured from vision until one was directly upon them. Many a violent swerve I made to avoid hitting unlighted vehicles. Thus, nervously we made our way through the night with Pastor Shu and Joseph sharing the cab with me. A couple who begged a ride with us were sandwiched into the rear, creating discomfort both for them and the team members.

Work had been done on the truck, and the new cylinders gradually adjusted themselves to the engine rhythm and in the process fouled up the timing. When we reached Tainan, midway to the southern tip of the island, I was no longer able to keep the engine running. I knew a bit about the little screw on the carburetor, which Rollie told me had something to do with timing, so with the aid of a flashlight I tinkered with it. Then I congratulated myself on the success of my operation. Though perhaps a little fast, the engine actually did keep running. I was pooped by the time we arrived in Kaohsiung. It was 11:00 p.m. and we had only gone about 100 miles.

The next morning we received the unhappy news that the road from Taitung to Hualien, the first major city on the east side, was out, thanks to a recent typhoon. We checked at the bus station, and they assured us that the road was still being used. Thus encouraged, we hurried on our way.

We soon rounded the southern tip of the island and started north via the coastal highway. Shortly after passing through Pingtung, we were again warned that the road from Taitung to Hualien was impassable. Nevertheless, we pressed on. Soon pavement ended and dirt road began. It was the last paved highway we were to see before our final destination.

The truck weaved crazily around the curves, clattering along a series of ruts, jiggling us the whole way. We eventually arrived in Taitung. Now we began to see tribal people clustered in small hollows among the hills. Their features are quite distinct from the Chinese and their standard of living much lower.

That evening we took a room in a local hotel and were immediately accosted by a bevy of beautiful women, the expected prostitutes of many of Taiwan's hotels. Their mannerisms set them distinctively apart from the usually shy and reserved Chinese women. They seemed offended that we declined their services.

The big question that we now faced was what, in fact, was the actual condition of the road to Hualien. Did the road even still exist? If so, where was it? Our inquiries concerning the entry point and condition of this highway were met with a variety of responses. Some assured us that the road was open but was exceedingly dangerous. Others were less hopeful and warned that it was completely washed out. Their advice was to ship the truck by the narrow-gauge railroad to Hualien.

We checked into this possibility but were put off by the cost of doing so, which was more than our crusade budget would allow. So while the rest of the team boarded the narrow-gauge train to continue the journey, Joseph and I set about finding the coastal highway.

We finally located the elusive road. At the start, it was smooth enough and shaded by tall trees on either side. It was a fine day, and the breeze from the coast made for very pleasant driving weather. The two of us were in a good mood and felt almost equal to anything that the fortunes of the day might present us with. The red truck was doing well and, after a second carburetor adjustment, it proceeded contentedly. This continued for the first half-hour.

Then came our entry to the mountains. The road became

perceptively narrower and rougher. That is when we remembered the stationmaster's caution. Suffice it to say that we later learned the road was almost never traveled in its entirety from Taitung to Hualien. I cannot recall the number of bridges that were washed out and the number of rivers we were forced to ford, but there were not a few. We plunged into water of unknown depth and maneuvered precariously up muddy embankments.

Seven times we had to get permission from local officials to use their bridges. At one stop, they told us we were the only ones who had driven that road the entire day. We understood why! When it was not descending into riverbeds or streams, the road was clinging to precipitous ledges. At one place, it was little more than a wide cow path with a washboard-like texture.

Most unnerving of all was the time we came suddenly to a rise that indicated the edge of a riverbed. Joseph cautioned me to reduce speed. A good thing too, because suddenly before our eyes the road vanished. It ceased to exist. It was just not there. I slammed on the brakes, and we skidded over rough gravel to a perilous halt. We were resting atop a small cliff. Ten feet more and we would have plunged down an embankment. We gave thanks, cautiously backed the truck up, and eventually found an alternate route.

Some weeks later a letter from Mother informed me that she had been awakened at night with a great urge to pray for me, sensing that I was in danger. This call to prayer, I discovered, happened at precisely the same time that our vehicle was approaching that precipice.

We continued. Our red truck with a foreigner at the wheel created quite a sensation wherever we went, and we were greeted by excited cries from children and queries from adults. The last river crossing was the worst. A truck driver warned us that his large, powerful vehicle had just barely made it. He thought ours would probably stall midstream but, typically, suggested we try it anyway. This was unsettling advice.

It was a wide river, perhaps seventy-five feet across with two swift branches. This called for an investigation. I took off my shoes and fought my way across the water until it was above my knees, high enough to flood the engine and halt our progress. We finally decided that, since we did not want to spend the night there, we would pray and proceed.

I backed up and gunned the motor. The truck created an impressive spray as we entered the water. There followed a few seconds of sputtering before our faithful vehicle rocked and lurched its way to the opposite bank. A great volley of gratitude rose from our still-trembling hearts.

Now our destination was just before us. Soon we were approaching the outlying districts of Hualien and then on to Chunghua Road, pulling up in front of a shabby-looking building. The boys came out with excited greetings. They had arrived well before us. Amazingly, in spite of the hazards, we had made it to Hualien.

Chapter 24

HUALIEN AND HONG KONG

The hall that the team captain had rented for us was uncommonly ill-suited to our needs. It was actually situated on the outskirts of town in the midst of lumberyards. At night, almost no one passed within sight of the hall, so our attempts to induce passersby to attend the meetings were useless. We spent the night in a hotel and the next day searched for a more suitable location. We found a storefront in a densely populated area of the city. The landlord, however, insisted on our paying six months' rent in advance, a sum of money which was reluctantly wrung from our field treasurer, Uri Chandler.

Before long, however, we discovered that there was an unforeseen problem. The building had no proper drainage. All wastewater was emptying into a smelly bog out in back where it created a small swamp. We finally resorted to employing a local plumber to put in a decent drain. This, of course, further strained our budget.

The cook that our local aboriginal church had hired for the crusade had her own standard of sanitation, which we discovered to be much at variance from that of the Taiwanese. She refused to clean the toilet and did little to keep our quarters in order. When we reminded her that the bedrooms were dirty, she smiled and remarked, "Well, you have your bedding to sleep on so that doesn't matter." As a cook, she had her own ideas about a proper diet, one which would never have passed the Betty Crocker test. The boys wanted to dismiss the woman but this we realized would have created some serious relational problems with the tribal church.

I had been in Hualien for a while before I saw my first fellow foreigners. On the edge of town, the Mennonites had erected an excellent and much-appreciated hospital. In other towns, missionaries had occasionally invited me to their homes. Here I especially appreciated the invitation to join foreigners for a marvelous American Thanksgiving dinner. These Mennonites were lovable people and were devoted to doing needful work in their excellent hospital.

My favorite of these folk was an open, warm-hearted missionary named Hans Vandenberg. He was a heavy-set and jovial Dutchman I had seen bounding around town on his motorcycle. Hans had a deep love for the people. He was all friendliness and had a hearty handshake and a kindly consideration and understanding of human nature. In ten minutes he told me more about the Taiwanese than I had learned in a year.

I still remember with fondness our months in Hualien, situated on the narrow eastern coastline, which opens to the famed marble-faced Taroko Gorge leading to some of Taiwan's highest mountains. The gorge is a majestic natural wonder. On our days off we would pile into the truck and become sightseers. Not far away was a beautiful lake on which was located a Presbyterian Bible school with seventy students. They gave us a sincere welcome and invited me to speak in a morning chapel.

One of my English students, Mr. Chen, would sit through our services, staid and dignified. I thought I detected something of disgust in his countenance but I was wrong. One day he told me simply, in halting English, "Sometimes I go to the mountains to talk to God. Sometimes I cry." So we met to talk about Jesus, faith, salvation, and the church. Before we left Hualien,

Mr. Chen had become a true friend. I later heard that he had received Christ and was attending the church.

Another student in the English class was a Cantonese and an office worker. He was delighted to meet an American and was intent on having frequent conversations in English. There came the beginning of openness to the gospel and almost immediately, it seemed, the man understood and invited Christ to be his Savior.

We do not always see conversions in this way. Usually the light breaks slowly, but here was a soul that God had been preparing and infusing with hunger for himself. Within two weeks he had given up drinking and smoking. He was in every Sunday morning service with a heavenly smile on his face. Soon he brought his wife, and with child-like eagerness urged her to believe in God.

Another interesting aspect of life on the East Coast and in the Hualien area is that the city is situated on a fault line. The result is frequent earthquakes, an average of ninety a year. While few of these are strong enough to level buildings or destroy roads, they did tend to keep us a bit on edge, wondering if the next one would be a historic, cataclysmic natural disaster.

Although the city of Hualien was occupied primarily by Taiwanese and mainland Chinese, the adjacent mountain areas were almost entirely the province of the aborigines, seven tribes which are scattered in upland areas.

On one occasion, shortly after our arrival, we witnessed sad and pathetic tribal festivities. Although many Amis are Christians, this celebration was decidedly a pagan one. It began with slow rhythmic dancing and some consumption of alcohol. Gradually, the pace quickened, eventually giving way to a full-fledged orgy. They made an attempt at friendship by urging us to drink a strange white alcoholic beverage with them. They were puzzled that we refused. Later they produced thick pancake-like loaves of bread. These we accepted and managed a few bites. The Ami women, if married, were adorned with black tattoos, running from the ear to the corner of the mouth. Many of them smoked crude wooden pipes.

Amazingly, during World War II, in the absence of all foreign missionaries, Japanese Christians had brought the gospel to these tribal people. The result was what is termed in missions "a peoples' movement." Nearly 80 percent of the mountain folk became Christians. As for the rest of Taiwan's people, the Chinese, only 5 percent professed faith in Christ.

The history of missions illustrates the fact that the more primitive a people, the more easily they are evangelized. Those like the Chinese, however, who have ancient traditions, sacred scriptures, and an organized system of religion going back thousands of years, are far less receptive to the gospel.

From time to time, I was invited to speak in one of the tribal churches with Joseph, who knew some Japanese and interpreted for me. The tribal pastor would translate from the Japanese into the tribal dialect.

While there are many fond memories of our crusade in Hualien, I also retain strong recollections of loneliness. On the West Coast, it was customary for me to return to the campus in Taichung every weekend to enjoy the company of fellow missionaries. In the remote East Coast area, I often felt very much alone with little contact with my own race and my own language.

Occasionally, I would take long walks along the coastline, jumping from rock to rock, praying in loud cries that I was sure would never be heard by others, thanks to the crashing of great breakers. I comforted myself with the thought that I was standing on the edge of the greatest ocean on earth, and it is the same ocean that touched the shores of my homeland.

On the final night of the Hualien crusade, there was an

attendance of almost ninety. It was an exciting and gratifying evening. Christmas was coming and my text was "There was no room for Him in the inn." I felt that the Lord mightily enabled me to talk above the incessant din of traffic and, despite the interruptions of an unhappy policeman, the Holy Spirit was powerfully working. Some fourteen people raised their hands that night to receive Christ. It was a beautiful benediction, far better than we deserved.

On the return trip, rather than braving the nearly impassable southern route, we headed north to Taipei along the coast road, a single lane with scheduled one-way traffic literally carved out of the high coastal cliffs. We reached Taipei the following evening, and the next day we were back in Taichung at the OMS Bible school campus.

That summer, Dale McClain, our field leader in Hong Kong and a longtime family friend, was invited to Taiwan as one of the main speakers for the church's annual conference, as well as being one of the speakers at the yearly summer missionary conference held in Taichung at Morrison Academy. On the seminary campus, he was housed in a room adjacent to mine, as I now had an apartment of my own.

In Dale I found a partner to help carry a prayer burden for the church. We would gab awhile and then share blessings. Then one of us would say, "Well, let's pray." We were so blessed, that we agreed that it was wrong to be selfish with this kind of blessing so we invited the entire missionary group to join us each noon for a time of fasting and prayer.

Later, an invitation came from both Dale and Florence Munroe, who were the founders of our work in Hong Kong, inviting me to speak at the OMS Hong Kong winter conference. That a missionary as youthful as me should be accorded this honor was quite overwhelming, but under the circumstances, I felt that I could do nothing but accept.

I had not seen Hong Kong since our return from India in 1949. Now even greater throngs of refugees were flooding the city to escape Mao Tse-tung's Communism. Hong Kong, still a British possession, seemed the only safe haven in China. It was, in fact, one of the most densely populated cities in the world with a population of about four million.

In a brief time, the refugee influx from the mainland had turned Hong Kong into a vast crush of human beings. I saw refugees everywhere on the sidewalks, living under crates or between slabs of tin and sleeping on straw mats. The government had built five-story H-block buildings, each housing twenty-five hundred human beings. Families were wedged into narrow concrete cells, five to a room.

This city was home to displaced Chinese with their own dialects from every province. Longtime residents of the British colony, if not speaking Cantonese, were talking English in a British or stilted Anglo-Indian accent, and among them were also tourists with a multiplicity of languages.

Upon arrival in December, I was treated to a tour of the city. We took the cable car up to the peak on Hong Kong Island and then to Aberdeen, the harbor festooned with junks and floating restaurants famous for seafood. Hong Kong is also one of the greatest shipping centers, boasting the world's most scenic harbor. In fact, the name *Hong Kong* in Chinese means "fragrant harbor."

With Christmas approaching, I stayed with my brother, Bob, and his wife, Phyllis, new arrivals in Hong Kong. They had recently become parents of a charming little son, Paul. Though I knew I was scheduled to speak to our missionaries and workers, I had no idea how many times I would speak. I asked Bob about this. He replied, "Well, two times on Sunday morning and then afternoon and evening services for a week, which makes about fourteen services or so." I thought he was kidding.

Fourteen services, I thought to myself. I am absolutely incapable of such an assignment! I complained, "Lord, I've come here for a vacation and will now have to work twice as hard as usual." That night I read Exodus 33: *My presence shall go with thee, and I will give thee rest* (KJV). All in all, those days, though strenuous, were a delightful interlude. Between services, we even managed a number of sets of tennis at the local British servicemen's club.

During my stay in Hong Kong, Gladys Aylward had been invited to speak at the mission prayer meeting. She had recently gained considerable fame as the heroine of the movie *The Inn of the Sixth Happiness*. With the approach of the Red Army, she had rescued nearly 100 orphans, leading them on a torturous trek across north China in order to escape to Taiwan. Meeting Gladys was for me a rare and unforgettable experience.

How do you describe this little woman? Yes, she was small. But surprisingly there was power in her manner, and her movements were energetic and decisive, giving us the feeling that here was someone who knew where she was going and no one had better try to stop her. She was fiery with an absolutely amazing dramatic instinct. She sat on a straight-back chair looking at each of us squarely and spoke in a sort of Cockney English.

After a few introductory remarks, she then fumbled around in her Bible for a verse. She started her message in a low voice. And then suddenly her eyes flashed and every mannerism spoke of dynamic life, a formidable flow of vitality. Her story was simple and contributed to the power of her message. And into the drama she wove the pathos of the lonely years in China, as recorded in her biography, *The Small Woman*. A woman without higher education, she was both an artist and a dramatist.

Being in the presence of Miss Aylward was a beautifully

spiritual experience. Very British, she was apparently not a great admirer of the United States. She had recently toured the U.S. and denounced the Yankees' luxurious mode of life and their shameless wealth, which she saw as mostly devoted to the satisfaction of their own appetites. "Americans spend more money on Revlon than a Chinese family lives on in a year," she informed us. "Americans, Americans," she went on, "so materialistic. I feel sorry for those Americans." Having spent a year away from the homeland and in the company of some of the poorest refugees on earth, I felt that this small woman was probably right.

When I returned from Hong Kong by boat, I was packing assorted bundles of articles not available in Taiwan. The missionaries had provided me with shopping lists, and Polly McClain, Dale's wife, knew every shop to go to in order to obtain the articles.

Back in Taiwan, Uri met me at the dock, emphasizing the importance of haste in order to get the express train to Taichung. As we passed through the turnstile at the railway terminal in Taipei with our loads of baggage, Uri saw that our train was already moving. Dropping his load of baggage, he sprinted across the platform and hopped on the nearest carriage, leaving me behind with a load of luggage and boxes of groceries. The train was swiftly disappearing.

What was I to do? Needless to say, I missed the train and spent several unhappy hours guarding my baggage before I managed to catch the late evening express.

CHAPTER 25

THE DELUGE

The Taiwan Holiness Church had determined to plant a church in Wufeng, a small town about half an hour's drive from Taichung and the seat of Taiwan's provincial capital. Chiang Kai-shek was adamant that the Republic of China (Taiwan) was the one and only rightful government of China, and, although every province except Taiwan was now in Communists' hands, Taipei was designated the national capital of China and Wufeng the provincial capital. The provincial government in Wufeng was furnished with large, impressive buildings and to this city the senators resorted and carried on the actual work of governing Taiwan.

At my suggestion, it was agreed that since Wufeng was close to Taichung, we could plant a church in Wufeng and at the same time assist a small congregation begun in South Taichung and now floundering badly.

The opening week of the South Taichung work was most encouraging. We had several decisions for Christ, but not until Sunday morning did I feel real liberty. There were two decisions that morning, one of them the former mayor's wife. In the evening service, Pastor Teh spoke and God blessed. A local newspaper reporter accepted Christ. He attended our services the first two nights and testified that his heart had been "strangely warmed," as John Wesley would have put it. Sunday afternoon we opened an instruction class for Christians who desired to help us in the crusade. I lectured on the fundamentals of personal evangelism. Thereafter, they began visiting and distributing gospel portions and tracts in adjacent areas.

In these summer months, part of the time I was in my quarters on the seminary campus and had added time for Bible study as well as for exploring some devotional classics. I started with a long-sought-for volume, *With Christ in the School of Prayer,* by Andrew Murray and also *The Pursuit of God* by A.W. Tozer, a book with amazing power and charm. For the second time I read Jonathan Goforth's *By My Spirit* and took careful notes. This was the answer for Taiwan, the outpouring of the Holy Spirit.

Our dual crusade had made a good start but was about to be interrupted. One night the heavens opened, and there came a deluge of rain such as few have ever experienced – torrents and torrents of unrelenting rain with no letup. This was accompanied by wave after wave of great peals of thunder along with continuous lightning.

The next morning I was scheduled to drive Joseph to the station. This, I soon learned, was beyond the realm of possibility. The lower end of the compound was under water and the streets of Taichung were barely discernible, having disappeared under wide, swirling rivers. Great numbers of people were now fleeing to higher ground, transporting with them what belongings they could carry. Some were taking refuge in our chapel which was located on higher ground. During that night, an unprecedented sixteen inches of rain had fallen, and many of the towns in the area had nearly disappeared as if under a tidal wave.

The situation was far worse in nearby Changhua, the epicenter of the terrible storm. Rail lines had completely washed out in several areas and most of the highways were impassable.

In downtown Changhua, within a matter of three minutes, the vast torrential floodwaters had risen from ground level to the second story of most buildings. Hundreds were drowned and their bodies swept away into gullies and small rivers, so plentiful in this mountainous island province. It would be days before it was possible for our team to return to the crusade sites.

We endeavored to keep in touch with those who had come to Christ. One afternoon we visited the newspaper reporter saved during the campaign. We found a still-radiant Christian and his wife, a most loquacious sister filled with wonder at the transformation in her husband. She decided that whatever it was that he had it was good. We talked to him about the new life and the necessity of growth and fellowship through the Word and prayer. Then we pointed out the conflicting life of the flesh which wars against the Spirit as described in Galatians chapter 5. Often in these dealings the Spirit would impress upon my mind just the passage I should use.

By the end of the summer, the Wufeng church was established after a fashion, and the attendance at the South Taichung church increased measurably.

It was about this time that it came to my attention that one of our most likable crusaders, Mr. Tan, had been secretly involved in some extracurricular activities. During the Touliu crusade, we had all noticed his increasing aloofness. Whereas before he was a most zealous Bible distributor and salesman, he now seemed distant and preoccupied. We guessed that some personal frustration had him worried.

The boys began to talk among themselves about his curious behavior. He was gone every afternoon during the rest period, supposedly to play ping-pong. He had been a champion player in the military.

Soon it all came out. A couple of our team members had observed Tan in the company of an unusually attractive young lady who had attended our services quite regularly. This would not have been a cause for great alarm were it not for the fact that Tan was married and the father of a three-year-old son.

During the intermediate period between the Touliu and Tainan campaigns, Tan had not even gone home to his wife and family nor had he communicated with his wife, but instead remained behind in Touliu. Late one night, his wife had appeared at the home of Joseph's parents in great distress of mind, inquiring the whereabouts of her husband.

Young as I was, I had never had to deal with problems of this nature. As a kind of de facto team leader, I now felt it was my responsibility to confront Mr. Tan. He claimed that he had to be separated from his wife since she was duty-bound to care for her aged parents living on the distant island of Penghu.

With Joseph as my interpreter, I tried my best to show him in light of the Scriptures the disastrous consequences of the sin in which he was so obviously entangled. I used Proverbs chapters 5 through 7, a powerful condemnation of adultery and the dangers of illicit relationships. The Scriptures showed better than I ever could what one must expect when he plays with that kind of fire. I told him frankly that if this conduct did not change he could expect immediate termination of his employment by the church and, worse, he would be answerable at the judgment seat of God.

He agreed to break off the relationship. I explained that it would be some months before we would allow him to preach in our services. The handsome and likable Mr. Tan, I'm glad to say, made a full recovery and years later proved an excellent pastor and one of the leaders of a denomination in which he served.

At this time, I reviewed my experiences as a rural evangelist and street preacher. One day I made note of all the Devil's methods that we had encountered in the process of spreading the gospel in rural Taiwan. The Devil has his strategies and devices for undoing the work of the Lord. One of these is the interruption of services and messages, just at the precise moment when a minister is bringing the issue of repentance to a climax. Satan loves to distract in some way the seeker's attention and deaden the growing conviction. Many times during our services, whether in the gospel hall or on city streets, some sort of disturbance would occur at the most inopportune moment. Here are a few instances.

1. As stated earlier, during a Sunday night service, a drunkard began asking irrelevant questions in a loud, harsh voice. Later, he rose and urinated on the floor.

2. During a South Taichung service, as I was bringing my message to a close, the pastor's kitten fell from the high banister, which led to the second floor, falling atop the blackboard where it played just long enough to distract everyone. From that point on, there was little use in continuing the message.

3. While on the street of Yuanlin, just as my message was coming to a conclusion, a grand funeral procession was heard approaching, accompanied by all manner of drums and other noisemakers. This continued for fourteen minutes, by which time most of our audience had left.

4. In another street meeting, a small boy strolled up and began energetically stomping on my foot to the amusement of everyone.

5. One morning in Wufeng, we were preaching in the marketplace to an audience of fifty or more. The people were listening intently. The message over, I got up to introduce Bibles for sale. I gave

my preliminary talk on the worth and value of the Word of God when I heard in the distance a loudspeaker coming down the street, apparently advertising scheduled movies showing in the local theater. Following the first cart blasting out the announcement was a three-wheeled conveyance carrying no fewer than eight showgirls, all dolled up. They were distributing movie leaflets to the onlookers. By the time the procession had passed, there were only four adults remaining in our audience.

6. In one city on Sunday mornings, about halfway through our service, the loudspeaker on the adjacent building would come on with a half-hour of raucous music, rendering preaching ineffective, if not impossible.

September 20 was the first anniversary of my arrival in Taiwan. I was far from being a veteran, as proven by my incredibly bad handling of the language. Yet I had acquired some familiarity with the customs and thinking of the people. It had been a good year and God promised more.

But, having been in Taiwan nearly a year and despite my busy schedule and ministry opportunities, I felt quite lonely. I had not had a friend of my own nationality and age to relate to since arriving. I was either a kid romping with Gary, Sheryl, and Gordie, or an adult having theological discussions and posing problematic issues over conference tables. Joseph was still with the team and proved a blessed companion in helping to fill some of my needs.

Chapter 26

CHANGHUA

Our next assignment was Changhua, a prominent city in the central part of the island, just south of Taichung, and a site of entrenched superstition. The city had erected the tallest (at that time) sitting Buddha in the world. The rotund image towering to a height of five stories looked on benignly and serenely over the occupants of the town.

Strangely, Changhua had also been one of the first Christian settlements since the dispersion of the Dutch and now boasted a prominent Christian hospital. The Holiness church in Changhua had been planted in the early 1950s. By 1959, however, this small church was on the wane and our church leaders feared it was in danger of extinction.

The hall in which we met and lived during this period was quite different, in that, instead of ordinary and indiscriminate cement walls, the church building was a visual pleasure. It had beautiful porcelain-tiled floors and walls, forming a wainscot. Even the light fixtures looked like they belonged in a well-appointed mansion. This puzzled me. How was it possible for the denomination, limited financially, to ever own such a building?

It was some weeks before I learned the answer to that question. In the late 1940s, the edifice had been constructed and occupied by a wealthy doctor who employed a young servant girl. Her responsibility was not only to care for the children but also to do a large part of the cooking and cleaning. Altogether, the task was far beyond her, but the doctor and his wife were not sympathetic. Shouts and threats, we were told, could be heard issuing from the building day and night.

Then one evening, after the doctor and his wife returned from a party for the more affluent of Changhua residents, upon opening the door, the street light fell across the form of a young girl dangling by her neck from the ceiling light fixture. Their poor servant, overworked and seeing nothing but torment in the future, had hung herself.

Not long after, it was reported that strange sounds were heard coming from this address and sometimes screams. When the couple was upstairs in bed at night, the sound of sweeping, which had been the primary task of the young girl, could be heard late into the night. Then occasionally footsteps were heard on the narrow stairway leading to the bedroom.

Thus, the premises were vacated and an attempt made to rent the house. By now, the rumors of haunting had spread far and wide. No one was interested in dealing with a ghost. After a long period of vacancy, ministers of our church appeared in town looking for a suitable place for a meeting hall. They heard rumors of haunting but dismissed the tales as foolish superstition. The price was incredibly low, and in a short time, the new pastor and his family had moved into this plush dwelling.

Some weeks later, as the pastor and his wife were in bed and on the verge of slumber, they were awakened by a strange sound of sweeping downstairs. Then followed footsteps approaching, walking up the narrow stairway toward their bedroom. There came a powerful and uncanny sense of a presence at the head of their bed. Both husband and wife testified to the feeling of hands upon their throats, gripping and tightening. It occurred to them that perhaps the talk they had heard about haunting was not all fable. The pastor remembered that in the Gospels it was the name of Jesus that had power over evil spirits.

Together he and his wife fell on their knees and began to cry loudly, "In Jesus' name! In Jesus' name!" demanding that the spirit leave. They again heard footsteps, this time going downstairs and then the sound of the back door slamming shut. This was curious because this door was always padlocked. When they examined it the next morning, the lock was still in its place and the door securely shut. They were never again troubled by ghosts or activity of any evil spirits.

It was into these quarters that our team moved, all of us sleeping in that same once-haunted bedroom on the very tatamis where the first pastor and his wife were assaulted by demonic spirits.

My English classes started with an unusually large attendance but soon uncharacteristically melted away to practically nothing. Nevertheless, the evening services were encouraging. The hall fronted one of the main thoroughfares which was crowded at night with scores of pedestrians. Our alert team members met and escorted people into the hall where many stayed for the entire service. At the conclusion, not only were hands raised for prayer, but there were also a number of definite conversions.

A young boy who worked as a coffin maker down the street from us drifted into the service one evening. He listened and the next night returned and received Christ as Savior. I will never forget the afternoon we visited him. It was growing dark outside, and only a small bulb in the back of the shop provided illumination, sending its eerie yellow shaft across the stacks of oval-shaped coffin boards. Here and there about us were caskets in various states of construction.

We were invited in and sat down opposite the young fellow. He was positively glowing. The new life impressed itself upon every feature of his face. It was as though some great power had been released within him. We talked to him about John 11:25, pointing out that the coffins spoke of a physical death, but for the Christian, death was only the doorway to eternal life.

On the other side of town, we visited a distinguished-looking lady. Her story was a sad one, yet typical of Taiwan. She had married, but upon arrival at her husband's home had discovered that he already had a wife. She was to be his concubine.

This enraged the woman and she turned in bitterness against the man who had treated her so cruelly. In time, he came to accept her shrewish behavior as a matter of course. Then came the great change.

One day he noticed that his second wife no longer seemed to harbor seeds of bitterness. Indeed, her whole attitude toward him had changed and she had a gentle and sweet spirit. What had happened? There was no accounting for such a change, not apart from the matchless Savior whom she had received into her heart after one of our services. We rejoiced together that our labor had not been in vain in this dark city steeped in demonic influence.

My English class now began to grow, with eight young people accepting the Lord as Savior. Across the street from us lived the Wangs. Both of their sons attended universities in Taipei. I first met the younger boy one evening. He asked when I would be preaching in English. As we talked, I discovered a heart that the Lord had been preparing for some time and felt certain that this young man would find the Lord.

In all crusades where foreigners are present, there are usually individuals who attend the services out of mere curiosity or a desire to make friends with foreigners. One such fellow, a young man of limited education but with a great talent for loquaciousness, began coming every night, primarily to argue with me. He first declared that he was an atheist and somewhat later a Buddhist and finally a Communist. At this time in Taiwan, it was decidedly unsafe to declare oneself a Communist. Most such zealots landed in jail or on a notorious prison island off the coast. So I was troubled when this professing Communist began attending our services. Whenever I saw him in the congregation, I knew I was again in for more harassing and argument.

One night, however, at the invitation this young man stood up. He was seated on the very back row and purposefully made his way down the aisle to kneel at the front bench. I was amazed. He was actually weeping, confessing his sins, and crying out to God for mercy. Thereafter, with great joy and enthusiasm, he declared himself a Christian and insisted on accompanying us on our daily street meetings and distributions of Scriptures. He wanted to tell everyone of his marvelous conversion. I named him Paul.

One day he went with us to small outlying villages in the area as the team passed out Scriptures, sold Bibles, and preached in the street. We had learned of a picturesque and famous temple not far away, so later that morning we decided to visit the site. The road to which we were directed, although initially wide and well maintained, turned increasingly narrow as it wended its way between rice paddies.

Soon it was apparent that we were definitely on the wrong road. This necessitated turning around, a feat almost impossible on the now nearly non-existent path that snaked its way through the rice paddies. Presently, however, we came to a broad flat area, which seemed the perfect place to turn around. We tested it and sure enough, it was plenty hard. I eased the truck onto the broad expanse of level dirt. Suddenly I was aware of a terrible dragging and sinking sensation as if I was driving with the brakes on. Then we came to a stop.

When I got out to investigate, I was alarmed to discover the running board almost level with the ground. A recent drought had baked the upper crust of the field nice and hard, but the weight of the truck was sufficient to break through the crust and deliver us into the depths of a squishy reservoir of mud.

It was about 11:00 a.m. when the incident occurred. After all of our pushing failed, we borrowed a pair of oxen and harnessed them to the truck. Unfortunately, the beasts were terrified by their proximity to the strange vehicle. We had an undependable jack, which had never served us well but we shoved it under the truck's axle supported by a small foundation of bricks. I gunned the motor, hoping desperately for some forward movement. The wheels merely spun until all of the bricks had disappeared deep into the slough. By this time, a crowd of spectators had become even larger. They were clearly enjoying the spectacle.

It was nearly four o'clock. We had been mired in the mud for five hours. All of our devices and attempts had resulted in nothing more than humiliation. At this point, our recent convert spoke up. He had heard us talk about prayer and how God wonderfully answers. He was puzzled that we were not praying. We had tried our human devices. They had failed. In our hearts, we were importuning God but not publicly.

When Paul proposed we pray, I felt a twinge of shame. Here I was the missionary, the one who actually believed in miracles and the kindness of a heavenly Father. Was He not concerned that His children were stuck in the mud? We were all exhausted, a sorry sight, with our clothing and limbs covered with mud from head to foot. I suggested to the boys that we gather around.

One by one, we pled to our God to deliver us. The next step, of course, must be to prove our faith and once more do what we had been attempting for hours. The boys prepared to push from behind. I jumped into the cab, turned the key, and on signal fervently cried, "Push!" Wonder of wonders, that old and so-implacable vehicle moved, first a few inches and then a foot. Incredibly, with a sudden lurch, it was out of the mud and solidly came to rest on a firm dyke which separated the fields.

In missionary meetings, people often ask us questions such as, "Have you ever seen anything supernatural? How about casting out of demons and other miraculous deeds?" In response, I have no qualms about describing to them the mud paddy of rural Taiwan and how the hand of God worked on our behalf.

Paul later studied in our Bible school, but his poor academic background brought this endeavor to an end. He then worked at various jobs. He wrote a book called *The Secret of World Peace*. It was never a bestseller. Undeterred, he created a lapel pin declaring "Jesus is Lord." Millions, I was told, were sold and distributed not only in Taiwan but all over the world.

Chapter 27

CHIAYI AND HOME

Our next and my final Taiwan crusade was scheduled for late spring in Chiayi. This was the largest town in south-central Taiwan and was the southern headquarters for both the Lutherans and Friends (Quakers). This provided me opportunities for fellowship with kind missionaries of other denominations.

The site the church leaders had chosen was determined by its rental price and our small budget. It was not on a main thoroughfare but rather a narrow side road, an area we later learned had a less-than-desirable reputation. Immediately adjacent to our chapel was a brothel that did a lively business. Attendance at the crusade was initially small. The English class attracted a few people, but most had no interest in the Christian religion.

However, memorable for me was Mr. Li, an officer in the local police department. He was one of the millions of Chinese military who had come to Taiwan in 1949. They were the defeated army, now permanently cut off from their families. In Taiwan, they found a very different China with a population that resented them and showed a great deal of animosity toward these mainlanders who, in turn, treated the local people with little respect.

Mr. Li, in his early forties, enjoyed the English class, and we would often talk together before he returned to his quarters. He was very diligent in reading the Bible I gave him and eventually showed a true interest in the Christian faith.

Despite the unsuitability of the location, more and more began to attend our evening meetings and the English class worked its magic, continuing to draw from all quarters of the city young men and a few women ambitious to master our difficult language.

Since Chiayi was within a reasonable driving distance from Taichung, on Monday, my day off, I would frequently drive to the campus for friendship and some good American food. A number of our team who lived in that same area would often travel with me.

One Tuesday afternoon we were journeying back to Chiayi in the increasingly decrepit red truck (which upon my departure would be consigned to the junkyard). Traveling at a good speed and enjoying conversation, we approached a large flock of geese. The birds were bunched together along the shoulder of the highway. A small boy, perhaps ten or twelve, was assigned the challenging task of managing these not-too-bright fowls. If a driver by accident should kill a chicken, he was obliged to pay for it. Not so, in the case of geese. No human, it was decided, could be expected to predict the behavior of these stupid, gangly birds.

As our truck approached the flock, a large goose, presumably the leader, made a sudden and totally unexpected left turn. Within seconds, the entire flock followed suit, and by the time we reached, them half the flock occupied the entire road in front of us. I uttered some appropriate cry and slammed on the brakes. In an instant, a dozen or more of them had disappeared under the wheels and carriage of our truck. Their lifeblood was turning the highway into a slippery red concourse. Nothing like this had ever happened to any of us before. My first thought was annoyance that this huge assembly of geese had not been properly managed and guided. Immediately I realized the unfairness of expecting a small boy to control these big birds.

By the time we had skidded to a halt, the small boy was weeping because according to law, he knew he was responsible for this mishap, and there would be trouble at home when it was discovered that a good number of the precious flock had perished. We got out of the truck and with assorted lamentations examined the scattered corpses and assessed the damage. All of us were moved by the plight of the small boy. I thought it appropriate that we recompense him for some of his misfortune. What we did was to purchase several of the deceased geese.

My teammates commended me on my tender and sympathetic heart, and at the same time, were delighted at the prospect of goose for supper. That night, indeed, we had the anticipated feast, but it was ruined for me since the cook determined to enhance the feast by adding quantities of squash to the great cauldron of boiled goose. Squash, the one vegetable I still cannot tolerate!

With the passing days, I realized with increasing excitement that my sojourn in Taiwan was swiftly coming to an end. I had lived with most of my team now for almost two years, a very, very long time to be with men who were often irritable due to being deprived of regular access to their wives and families. Nevertheless, for the most part we had enjoyed an amiable friendship that would stand the test of time.

I knew it was customary for the foreigner to give gifts to friends and colleagues upon departure. My meager salary of less than $100 per month ruled out the possibility of purchasing any gifts that would truly be appreciated by the team. So instead I decided to bestow upon the boys almost every item of my clothing, apart from that required for the trip home. This was long before Taiwan had built great acres of factories and mills producing enough garments to clothe half of the world. American clothes were then viewed as products of supreme value.

I gathered the team together one afternoon and piled the clothing on my bed. I urged them one by one in turn to select an item of clothing until the whole heap was gone. Admittedly, most of the clothing was a little too large but that posed no problem for them. Items that did not fit could easily be altered by their nimble-fingered wives. It was a glad and happy time, and more than adequate words of appreciation were expressed.

Now I was literally counting the days until I would be with Rachel again. This inspired a poem.

> *Behold, behold with me, my love*
> *The long grey night is almost gone*
> *And out across the sky is flung*
> *The broad new banners of the dawn.*
>
> *An age ago we stood alone*
> *Upon the verge of night*
> *And poured upon our aching lips*
> *Last tender tokens of delight.*
>
> *And burning in our bosoms lay*
> *Unspoken hopes, unspoken fears*
> *And there we wept when first we looked*
> *Across the awesome toll of years.*
>
> *But that was all an age ago*
> *Now look the morning cometh soon*
> *And from the calendar we tear*
> *A last pale solitary moon.*
>
> *Now in the fragrant morning air*
> *The last faint trace of night will pass;*
> *I come to you, my sweet, I come*
> *With love, to claim my own at last.*

Usually upon the departure of colleagues, there is an appropriate farewell. Mine was warm and wonderful. Favorite dishes were on the menu, especially those that fellow missionaries had discovered early on that I loved. Then came kind words, prayers, and assurances that my return to Taiwan would be greatly anticipated. The day before my departure, Uri accompanied me to Taipei and the airport. The following morning we took a taxi to the simple airfield at the end of Nanching Lu. The plane was a new model, only recently put into service. It combined the benefits of a prop plane and the speed and power of the jet, and it was designated a prop jet. It was in service only a few years before all trans-Pacific planes were fully powered by large jets.

I was not originally scheduled to return home until fall, but the OMS committee had invited me to be one of the speakers at the annual convention held in Winona Lake in June. I also would be speaking in various churches and at camp meetings that summer.

In those days, most of the OMS staff was located in Los Angeles at our world headquarters. Each summer we drove in non-air-conditioned cars the four-day journey to Winona Lake, Indiana. I traveled with Mom and Dad, accompanied by Stan Dyer, a veteran crusader from Japan. We had a delightful time, stopping one night in beautiful Rocky Mountain National Park and Estes Park. I was in Winona Lake just long enough to unload baggage, and the same evening I drove three hours to Findlay, Ohio, to pick up Rachel.

At the conclusion of the Winona Lake convention, Rachel and I returned to Findlay for our wedding on July 9, 1960. I asked two of my former Asbury roommates, Earl Andrews and Stan Lawrence, to be my groomsmen. My sister, Vangie, and Rachel's nieces, Ann and Donna Bishop, were her attendants. At the reception, we had the opportunity to give testimony to God's gracious working in our lives.

Thanks to the generous invitation of friends W.L. and Beulah Smith, we spent our honeymoon in Ontario, Canada, on the banks of lovely Magnetawan Lake. We could not have dreamed at that time that one day our son Stuart would marry a member of Beulah Smith's family.

That fall I returned to Asbury Theological Seminary as a junior, which is the second year of a three-year course of study. Rachel had her degree in teaching and found employment in a small nearby school, Camp Dick Robinson, where students were drawn from rural Kentucky. She looks back at that initial teaching experience as a very happy time. When asked what she was doing, she would tell people she was getting her Ph.T. – **P**utting **H**ubby **T**hrough. After graduating from seminary with an MDiv, we spent a year in Los Angeles where I studied at UCLA and received a master's degree in journalism in the spring of 1963.

The following years led to a half-century of our lives together, serving in Asia and the United States.

Above: Taiwan, 1958: Crusade team

Right: Yuanlin with John and Samuel Chang

Below: Ed and Joseph Wang by the red crusade truck

Left: Daniel Chang, 1960

Right: Touliu, 1959: Mildred Rice and team members with new converts

Left: Relaxing

Left: Hualien, 1959: Crusade farewell meeting

Right: Aboriginal tribeswoman with child

Left: Beloved Amis tribe Pastor Wu

Left: Changhua Buddha

Right: Transportation of pig doing flood of 1960

Left: Married, July 9, 1960

Above: To Taiwan August, 1964, with Stephen

Above: To Taiwan 1975, Stuart, Rachel, Scott, Steve, Sharon, Ed

Above: Radio English Class, 1970s: Daniel Chang, Christine Helsby, Ed

Right: Departing for furlough

Left: With colleagues at Chung Tai Seminary, 1981

Right: With Ruth Chang and former English students, 2004

Left: As Asbury College representatives, 1991

Right: With Hong Kong colleagues, 1995

Left: Teaching in the Philippines, 1998

Above: Return visit to Taiwan, 2004, with Carol and Daniel Chang

Above: Return visit to Philippines, 2009

Above: English class baptism, 2006, with Chinese church members

Above: With family, 2012: Sam, Linda, Stuart, Luke, Ada, Scott, Ed, Wesley, Rachel Erny; Sharon, Morgan, Taylor, Kraig Binkerd; Eli, Christine, Caroline Erny

Right: 50th wedding anniversary, July, 2006

Left: Ed Erny

EPILOGUE

By Rachel Erny

This book is the first volume of my husband's autobiography, which he wrote before his sudden death on October 19, 2013. He was in good health and active with no apparent physical problems. The heart attack took him quickly, and he did not suffer. I'm grateful for the fifty-three years we had together.

With the help of my son Scott, I finished editing and proofing and published this part of his life story in 2015. Since he cannot write "the rest of the story," I will fill you in briefly on the ministry God blessed us with during the ensuing years.

My horizon was first broadened when Ed and I moved to California after he finished seminary. As he studied at UCLA, I taught in a Los Angeles middle school with a racial mix of African-Americans, Asians, and Caucasians. This was a new cultural experience for me.

Having spent nearly two years in Taiwan, Ed felt led to return there. We arrived in September 1964. Stephen, our oldest, had been born in March, so he had his six-month birthday on board ship.

I discovered that sub-tropical weather produces things unknown in temperate climates, especially mold on clothes hanging in closets, a profusion of insects (cockroaches and ants) that multiply astronomically, and continual sweating.

But the hardest adjustment was learning the language. Soon we began four hours a day of classroom instruction. We studied Taiwanese for two years, first in Taipei, the capital city, and then in Taichung where our mission work was centered. Later, we also pursued Mandarin, now the official dialect of all Chinese.

I came to realize, however, that the greatest barrier was the spiritual darkness. Satan does not give up territory easily, especially among a people whose history dates back five thousand years.

After two years, the three of us moved to Chiayi and helped Pastor Chen and his family in the church there. These were good days of cultural adjustment under their gracious guidance. The year before our first furlough, we moved back to Taichung and both of us taught in our seminary. Sharon, our second child, was born in November of that year, 1967.

After a year of home assignment, living with my mother in Findlay, Ohio, we returned to Taichung, teaching again in the seminary. By this time, Daniel Chang, who accepted Jesus when Ed was in the crusade ministry, came to the seminary as an interpreter. The two of them felt led to establish an English evangelism ministry, with night classes, a Sunday afternoon English rally, and daily teaching on the radio. There were also outreaches in other major cities of Taiwan that missionary colleagues led. On Sunday nights, a discipleship ministry for new converts was begun. It was held on the third floor of the English Ministries building, so it was called "The Upper Room."

In 1970, we welcomed our third child, Scott, and in 1972, our fourth, Stuart. The following year my mother died, my father having died shortly after I was married. It just was not possible for me to return to the States to attend her funeral. I was comforted knowing that my siblings would handle things well.

These were busy years with involvement in the English evangelism outreach, the seminary, the church, and the activities of our children at Morrison Academy. We experienced packing and unpacking, monsoons and typhoons, personnel problems and many guests, as well as wonderful fellowship with our missionary and national colleagues.

Living on a compound, which was the OMS Bible school campus, provided an oasis from the noisy and crowded city streets and a worry-free playground for our children. Also, living in Taichung, we were near the missionary school, Morrison Academy, with grades kindergarten through twelve. Being on a campus made us and our home very accessible. I truly learned to have an open-door policy and had many ministry moments with students.

I was blessed to have a reliable and sensible Taiwanese gal to help me in the home. She became like a member of the family. One day after she had mopped the stairs leading to the bedrooms on the second floor, she was extremely upset when the kids came marching in and left dirty marks on the steps. I knew then she felt like an older sister contending with younger siblings! As she grew in her faith, we had weekly devotions together and with other workers on the compound.

The English evangelism work proved to be very fruitful and fulfilling. In 1985, we left Taiwan to return to the U.S. for what we expected to be a year of furlough.

However, before this time, on February 19, 1984, we experienced the greatest sorrow of our lives. We received news that our son Stephen, a sophomore at Asbury College, had died. What added to the burden of his death was that he had chosen to end his life. Steve had been with us two months before, having come to Taiwan for his Christmas break. There was no indication of problems, as he was doing well in his studies, had many friends, including a special lovely lady, and expressed his love and appreciation for the family.

Ed and I made a hurried trip to the U.S. for his funeral and burial. Even to this day, it is very difficult for me to think of this great loss. The words from Isaiah 53:3, in the prophecy concerning Jesus, are meaningful: *a man of sorrows, and acquainted with grief* (KJV). God did comfort us through His love and the prayers and support of many, but Steve's presence will always be missed and his death a mystery.

During our furlough in 1985, we located in Greenwood, Indiana. Unexpectedly at this time, Ed was chosen to be the OMS president, and he served in that position from 1986 to 1991. Sharon entered college that fall at Taylor University in Upland, Indiana. The two boys had to make a big adjustment into American middle and high schools, a difficult challenge.

There were some knotty issues that had to be dealt with while Ed was in office, including financial needs and personnel problems on two of our fields, but by far, the hardest issue was a moral failing of a missionary that affected a number of people, causing much pain to those involved.

Ed began to experience depression, very much reminiscent of the emotional malady that his mother had known. It seems that creative people often have a tendency toward melancholy, which makes them more susceptible to this kind of illness. This was a very fearful time for me. We were finally able to get good medical help, which brought relief, but Ed realized he would need to be aware of and deal with this issue for the rest of his life. Taking up watercolor painting proved to be a wonderful therapy.

In 1991, we were assigned as OMS reps to students at Asbury College and Seminary. By this time, our daughter, Sharon, had graduated from college and was married to Kraig Binkerd. They live in Anderson, Indiana, where her husband teaches math in the local high school, while Sharon does counseling. Scott and Stuart were both studying at Asbury.

The contact with students was rewarding, introducing them to missions, having Bible studies, and "being a home away from home." The marriage of our two sons and welcoming the first grandchild were memorable events during this time!

In the summer of 1995, we moved to Hong Kong to fill in for furloughing missionaries. It was good to be back in Asia and again teaching English classes, working alongside our pastors in several churches. We did study a bit of Cantonese but were grateful for the British influence in that colony which meant that all the signs were bilingual. It was truly a user-friendly place to live.

When our year there was finished, we heard of a need for a Bible school teacher in the OMS work in the Philippines. So in 1996, we moved to Manila, a place I said I would never live because it was too hot. Ed had a wonderful teaching ministry, and the Filipinos were a warm-hearted people, as were our missionary colleagues. And, the best part, English was still in great use as it had been the national language for a number of decades. We studied Tagalog, but the peoples' English was much better than our language acquisition would ever be. Our six years there were very rewarding.

In 2002, we packed our things and moved to Indiana, returning to the Philippines to teach at Faith Bible College for part of the following school year. Back in the States, over Thanksgiving weekend of 2003, we moved into our "own" home, a condo across from the OMS headquarters. Having lived in mission property and rented dwellings since our marriage, it was a relief to know that no matter where we went, we would return to this place and didn't need to pack and unpack a whole household anymore.

After leaving the Philippines, we made several short-term trips overseas to teach. Ed continued to write missionary biographies, and we also had English classes for Chinese living in the area.

Our three children and their spouses and the eight

grandchildren all live in Indiana, such a blessing to us (and a continual blessing for me) as we enjoy times together.

Without so many friends, supporters, and our loving family, all that God enabled us to do would not have been possible. How grateful I am for His kindness and mercy. One of our richest possessions is the multitude of friends all over the world: missionary colleagues and national co-laborers too numerous to name, converts, students, friends and supporters, a loving family – how rich I am. My reality is Jesus' words in Matthew 19:29: *And everyone who has left houses or brothers or sisters or father or mother or children or fields for my sake will receive a hundred times as much and will inherit eternal life.*

Rachel Erny
Greenwood, Indiana
2014

About the Author

Ed Erny and his wife, Rachel, served as One Mission Society missionaries for more than forty years. They ministered in Taiwan, Hong Kong, and the Philippines. Dr. Erny graduated from Asbury University and Asbury Theological Seminary and received an MS in journalism from UCLA. In 1987, he was awarded an honorary doctorate from his alma mater, Asbury University. Dr. Erny passed away in October 2013.

Young Men of the Cross is the story of One Mission Society's commitment to do something never before attempted—to place the Gospel message in every home in a nation. Their target was Japan, which at the time had 10.4 million homes. The Great Village Campaign was launched in 1913 with young Japanese evangelists carrying Scriptures to thousands of homes on small islands, in dense forests, and across barely accessible mountain ranges. In 1917, ten young men from God's Bible School in Cincinnati volunteered to work with the Japanese evangelists to complete this monumental task.

The Second Crusade, a sequel to *Young Men of the Cross*, tells of One Mission Society's post-World War II attempt to again reach every home in Japan with the gospel. This time, the program was called the Every Creature Crusade (ECC, now known as Every Community for Christ), and young college students joined national coworkers in spreading the gospel in Japan. Later, crusaders were sent to Korea, Taiwan, and Hong Kong to take the ECC program to those OMS fields as well. One OMS leader said of the effect of the ECC in his life: "As our crusade team moved from town to town and witnessed the salvation of hundreds and the planting of scores of churches, it was this more than anything else that drew many of us back to those fields as career missionaries."

Missionary life is not what most people expect. One Mission Society missionary Millie Young shares in her biography, *Hidden Treasures*, that it is so much more than just preaching. Making daily contact, organizing camps, running Christian schools, and living among the people are vital components of ministry. It is letting the local people see you living your life, overcoming obstacles, and laughing. Millie experienced hardship and provision, joy and heartbreaking sadness, insurmountable obstacles and immense success in spreading the salvation message to the lost—especially in the rural areas of Colombia. Her missionary work is the living legacy of changed lives.